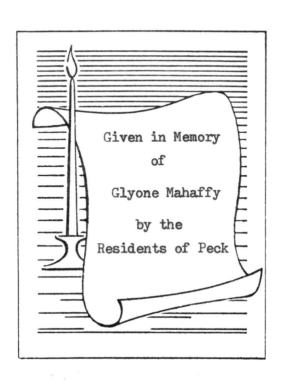

Given in Memory
of
Glyone Mahaffy

by the
Residents of Peck

THE POETRY OF
WILLIAM BUTLER YEATS

An Introduction

LITERATURE AND LIFE: BRITISH WRITERS

Complete list of titles in the series available from publisher on request. Some titles are also in paperback.

THE POETRY OF
WILLIAM
BUTLER
YEATS
An Introduction

William H. O'Donnell

UNGAR • NEW YORK

Copyright Acknowledgments

Poems by W. B. Yeats are reprinted by permission of
Michael B. Yeats and Macmillan London, Ltd. and of
Macmillan Publishing Company from *The Poems: A New
Edition,* by W. B. Yeats, ed. Richard J. Finneran. Copyright
1912, 1916, 1919, 1924, 1928, 1933, 1934 by Macmillan
Publishing Co., Inc. renewed 1940, 1944, 1947, 1952, 1956,
1961, 1962 by Bertha Georgie Yeats. Copyright 1940 by
Georgie Yeats, renewed 1968 by Bertha Georgie Yeats,
Michael Butler Yeats and Anne Yeats.

1986
The Ungar Publishing Company
370 Lexington Avenue, New York, N.Y. 10017

Copyright © 1986 by The Ungar Publishing Company

Printed in the United States of America

Library of Congress Cataloging-in-Publication Data

O'Donnell, William H., 1940–
　The poetry of William Butler Yeats.

　(Literature and life series)
　Bibliography: p.
　Includes index.
　1. Yeats, W. B. (William Butler), 1865–1939—
Criticism and interpretation.　I. Title.　II. Series.
PR5907.034　1986　　　821′.8　　　86-16048
ISBN 0-8044-2671-6

To my wife

Contents

Chronology

1865	William Butler Yeats is born June 13th in Dublin; he is the first of five children of John Butler Yeats (1839–1922) and Susan Mary (née Pollexfen) Yeats (1841–1900).
1867	Yeats family moves to London (until 1881); they spend frequent holidays in Sligo with Mrs. Yeats's family.
1881	Family moves to Dublin. Yeats attends Erasmus Smith High School, Dublin, until 1883.
1884–86	Yeats studies drawing at the Metropolitan School of Art and the Royal Hibernian Academy.
1885	His first poems are published. George Russell, Charles Johnston, and Yeats found the Dublin Hermetic Society. Yeats meets the Irish patriot John O'Leary.
1886	His first book, *Mosada,* a dramatic poem, is published. Family moves to London in April.
1887	Yeats joins Madame Blavatsky's Theosophical Society (until 1890).
1888	He begins editing collections of Irish folklore and of Irish fiction. He meets William Morris.
1889	His first collection of poems, *The Wanderings of Oisin and Other Poems,* is published. He falls in love with Maud Gonne (1866–1953).
1890	He joins the Hermetic Order of the Golden Dawn (until 1922). He is a founding member

of the Rhymers' Club and meets Lionel Johnson.

1891   *John Sherman and Dhoya* (novel and a short
        story) is published. T. W. Rolleston and he
        found the Irish Literary Society in London.

1892   Yeats goes to Dublin and begins two years of
        active campaigning for Irish cultural nation-
        alism, dividing his time between Dublin, Sligo,
        and London. He founds the National Literary
        Society in Dublin with support from John
        O'Leary. *The Countess Kathleen and Various
        Legends and Lyrics,* his nationalistic play and
        a collection of poems, is published.

1893   A three-volume edition and interpretation of
        Blake by Yeats and Edwin Ellis is published.
        Yeats's folklore collection, *The Celtic Twi-
        light,* is published.

1894   His play *The Land of Heart's Desire* is per-
        formed in London. He is introduced to Lady
        Gregory (1852–1932) in London. He meets
        Constance Gore-Booth (later Countess Mar-
        kiewicz, 1868–1927) and Eva Gore-Booth at
        their family home, Lissadell, near Sligo.

1896   He takes rooms in 17 Woburn Buildings,
        Bloomsbury (until 1917); he has an affair with
        Olivia Shakespear (1863–1938). He pays a brief
        call on Lady Gregory at Coole Park. He signs
        a contract for a novel, *The Speckled Bird.* He
        meets John Synge (1871–1909) in Paris.

1897   *The Secret Rose* (stories) is published. He
        spends his first summer at Coole Park. Lady
        Gregory, Edward Martyn, and Yeats plan the
        Irish Literary Theatre; George Moore joins
        them later. Maud Gonne and Yeats raise funds
        for a memorial to Wolfe Tone, leader of the
        1798 Rising.

1899   *The Wind among the Reeds* (poems) is pub-

lished. His play *The Countess Cathleen* is performed in the first of three annual seasons of
the Irish Literary Theatre in Dublin.

1902   Yeats's play *Cathleen ni Houlihan* is produced
in Dublin with Maud Gonne in the title role;
its success spurs the founding of the Irish National Theatre Society, with Yeats as president.

1903   Maud Gonne marries Major John MacBride;
they separate in 1905. Yeats publishes *Ideas
of Good and Evil* (essays) and *In the Seven
Woods* (poems and a play), which is the first
book printed by the Dun Emer Press (after
1908, the Cuala Press). Hugh Lane begins to
campaign for a gallery of modern art in Dublin. Yeats lectures in the United States and
Canada.

1904   Yeats continues his active leadership of the
Irish National Theatre Society, which opens
the renovated Abbey Theatre.

1907   John Synge's *The Playboy of the Western World*
causes an uproar at the Abbey Theatre. Yeats
tours northern Italy with Lady Gregory and
Robert Gregory. John Butler Yeats leaves for
New York, where he stays until his death in
1922.

1908   The elegant, eight-volume *Collected Works*
is published. Dublin Municipal Gallery of
Modern Art opens at a "temporary" site in
Harcourt Street, where it remains until 1933.

1910   *The Green Helmet and Other Poems* (play and
poems) is published.

1911   Yeats visits the United States with the Abbey
players.

1913   Yeats publishes *Poems Written in Discouragement,* centering on the Hugh Lane Gallery
controversy and other public events. Ezra

Pound is secretary to Yeats during the winters of 1913–14, 1914–15, and 1915–16.

1914   Yeats lectures in the United States and Canada. *Responsibilities* (poems) is published.

1916   Yeats publishes *Reveries over Childhood and Youth* (autobiography). *At the Hawk's Well*, the first of Yeats's Noh-style plays, is performed in London. The Easter Rising leads to the execution of Maud Gonne's estranged husband, Major John MacBride, in May. Yeats spends much of the summer with Maud Gonne in France. He arranges to purchase Thoor Ballylee.

1917   He takes possession of Thoor Ballylee and begins its renovation. Iseult Gonne (1894–1954) refuses his proposal of marriage in August. In October he marries Georgie Hyde-Lees (1892–1968). *The Wild Swans at Coole* (poems) is published by the Cuala Press.

1918   He moves to Oxford. Robert Gregory is killed in World War I. Yeats spends the summer near Coole, overseeing the renovation of Thoor Ballylee. *Per Amica Silentia Lunae,* essays on his theory of the mask, is published.

1919   His daughter, Anne Butler Yeats, is born in February, in Dublin. An expanded version of *The Wild Swans at Coole* is published by Macmillan. Yeats spends the summer at Thoor Ballylee. (Anglo-Irish War, 1919 through December 1921)

1920   Yeats lectures in the United States and Canada. After a brief visit at Thoor Ballylee he returns to Oxford.

1921   *Michael Robartes and the Dancer* (poems) is published. Michael Butler Yeats is born in August, in England. *Four Plays for Dancers* is published.

1922   Yeats moves to 82 Merrion Square, Dublin. He spends the spring and summer at Thoor Ballylee (also summers of 1923, 1926, and 1927). *The Trembling of the Veil* (autobiography) is published. He is appointed to the Senate of the Irish Free State (until 1928). (Irish Civil War, June 1922 through May 1923)

1923   Yeats is awarded the Nobel Prize for Literature.

1925   He visits Sicily and Italy. The first edition of *A Vision* is printed (issued in January 1926).

1927   He spends February and March in Rapallo, Italy. He suffers from congestion of the lungs in October and spends the winter of 1927–28 in Spain and the south of France.

1928   Yeats publishes *The Tower* (poems). He spends the spring in Rapallo, where he plans to make his permanent winter residence; he is there the winters of 1928–29 and 1929–30. In Dublin he moves to a flat at 42 Fitzwilliam Square.

1929   In December, at Rapallo, he is gravely ill with Maltese fever.

1931   He spends long periods at Coole Park with Lady Gregory until her death from cancer in May 1932.

1932   Yeats moves to the Dublin suburb of Rathfarnham. *Words for Music Perhaps* (poems) is published by the Cuala Press. He lectures in the United States and Canada.

1933   *The Winding Stair and Other Poems* is published.

1934   He has a Steinach rejuvenation operation.

1935   *A Full Moon in March* (poems and plays) is published. *Dramatis Persona* (autobiography) is published.

1936   He spends the winter and spring in Palma, Majorca, with Shri Purohit Swami, translating

	Upanishads; Yeats is very seriously ill in January, but recovers by April.
1937	The revised edition of *A Vision* is published.
1938	Yeats spends January to March in the south of France. *New Poems* is published by the Cuala Press. He goes to the south of France for the winter.
1939	Yeats dies on January 28th at Cap Martin, France. The Cuala Press posthumously publishes *Last Poems and Two Plays* and *On the Boiler* (essays, poems, and a play).
1948	Yeats's body is reinterred at Drumcliff churchyard, Sligo.

1

~~~~~~

A Poet's Life

William Butler Yeats is usually ranked as the greatest
poet of the twentieth century. Even so, some Irish wits
are convinced that Yeats would have been even better
if he had spent some time in pubs. The Irish enjoy a
good story, and an edge of delightful malice only adds
to the enjoyment. Several amusing anecdotes about Yeats
deal with his aloof, aristocratic demeanor. And one of
those stories tells of his only excursion into an Irish pub.
No witnesses survive today, but according to one—probably reliable—version, the poet was at least sixty years
old when he announced to a friend, Fred Higgins, "I
have never been in a pub in my life and I'd like to go
into a pub." Higgins carefully selected a Dublin pub that
he hoped would not offend Yeats's refined sense of pro-
priety. When the great moment came, Higgins took charge
of Yeats and prudently ordered mild drinks. Yeats looked
around for a moment and then announced, as his first
and last words in an Irish pub, "Higgins, I don't like it.
Lead me out again."[1]

Instead of the informality of a pub, Yeats consistently preferred a careful dignity, which was enhanced
by his striking physical appearance. His height of six foot
and one inch, his lanky build, and his thin face all contributed to an ethereal, artistic image that Yeats cultivated all his life. Simply put, he thought that a poet
should look like a poet. To call attention to his very long,
artistic fingers, he wore a large gold ring on the little
finger of his left hand. The artist who designed the ring

and who knew Yeats for many years aptly described Yeats's
thick, tousled black hair as "beautifully untidy."[2] In nearly
every photograph and portrait, a long lock of hair sweeps
down over his left brow. Until he was fifty he wore a
huge, flowing tie that had been the accepted emblem of
artists and poets during his youth. And when he finally
switched to a conventional bow tie, he was careful to
knot it loosely enough to hint at its artistic predecessor.

His acquaintances testified unanimously to the powerful effect of this carefully calculated pose during all of
his adult life. When Yeats was in his twenties, a young
woman reported, "In looks, Mr. Yeats is as picturesque
as one could desire. . . . Nature has written the poet
upon his face."[3] Similar comments are available during
each of the remaining decades of his life. In his thirties
he was admiringly described as the "very poet in appearance," in his forties as "the visible embodiment of
the poet," in his fifties as "gallantly attired" and looking
"very much like the poet he was," and, in the year he
turned seventy, as "an overgrown art student"—even to
the unsympathetic eyes of a brash young poet, Stephen
Spender, who disliked Yeats's politics.[4]

The Irish writer Padriac Colum recalled that Yeats's
pose challenged a viewer all the more because Yeats
believed in it so completely. Alvin Langdon Coburn, an
artistic young photographer, judged that Yeats's manner
in 1908 "would have been a pose in anyone else, but
with him it was quite natural, for Yeats was a real poet."[5]
That opinion was shared even by artists whose success
as caricaturists depended on a sharp eye and keen insight
into character. One caricaturist said, "It isn't a pose, it's
the man"; the other, who was a friend of Yeats's for
twenty-five years, observed, "There is a difference between acting a part for the benefit of an audience and
living it for the sake of one's soul."[6] Yeats often objected
to his treatment at the hands of ordinary portrait painters,
but he apparently enjoyed caricature portraits of himself,

probably because caricatures invariably emphasized the emblematic details of his physical appearance that he so carefully labored to bring to public attention.

As is suggested by Yeats's attention to looking the part of a poet, the single most important element in his life was his unwavering dedication to his career as a writer. But his shyness and reserve were at odds with the writer's necessity to face an audience: Yeats made repeated attempts at direct, public action. Some of those attempts are evident in his writing—for example, his enthusiasm for popular ballads and for plays. Other attempts were outside his artistic work, such as his Irish nationalist political involvements, which ranged from a brief membership in a secret revolutionary group to his service as an Irish Free State senator. In his efforts to foster Irish cultural nationalism he organized societies to support Irish literature; he helped to found an important Irish theatrical company and worked very actively as its president for many years. He lobbied for a gallery of modern art in Dublin and took part in a lengthy public controversy over some of its pictures. In old age Yeats wrote essays filled with vitriolic advice to the public. Those successive forays into public life each ended with frustration and a return to his native privacy, but he never was free of the urge for public involvement.

In nearly all of those public roles Yeats sought to enliven Irish culture and to make it more sophisticated. His Irishness was much more than a mere coincidence of his Irish birth, in Dublin on June 13, 1865. That sense of nationality was complicated because he belonged to the Protestant, Anglo-Irish minority. They had controlled the economic, political, social, and cultural life of Ireland since at least the end of the seventeenth century, but nearly all of them considered themselves as much English as Irish. The center of their world was not Dublin, but London, where Yeats lived for fourteen years during his childhood and where he maintained a per-

manent home throughout the full first half of his adult
life.

His father, John Butler Yeats, had graduated from
Trinity College, Dublin, in 1862 and had begun to study
law when he married Susan Pollexfen. She was the quiet,
eldest daughter of a prosperous partner in a milling company and shipping firm at Sligo, on the northwest coast
of Ireland. John Butler Yeats had a modest income from
some heavily mortgaged family lands and was a respect-
able, promising young husband, despite his free-thinking
views on religion. Then in 1867 he gave up law, began
a new career as a painter, and moved his family to London, where he enrolled in art school. Thus W. B. Yeats
spent his boyhood in London, but in some ways that
exile intensified his Irishness. During the family's long
holidays in Sligo he felt the strong contrast between
smoky London neighborhoods and picturesque Sligo. Yeats
often said Sligo was his real home, and he loved its
beautiful river, the nearby beach and lake, and the im-
posing bulk of the mountain Ben Bulben in the background.

Yeats's father was a powerful force in his son's life.
John Butler Yeats was a brilliant talker, and his love of
highly dramatic moments in literature certainly contributed to the son's lifelong interest in drama. The father's
strongest influence, however, was his absolute loyalty to
art. He expressed that commitment frequently in conversation and through his sublime casualness about the
family's day-to-day financial difficulties that resulted from
the meager sales of his paintings and drawings. Art became increasingly important in the son's life, especially
after the family moved back to Ireland in 1881. The
sixteen-year-old Yeats frequented his father's Dublin stu-
dio, which was known as much for John Butler Yeats's
lively talk as for his portrait painting. In 1884, at age
nineteen, W. B. Yeats enrolled in the Dublin Metro-
politan School of Art, where both his younger sisters

already were students. He soon tired of making drawing after drawing of plaster casts of Greek and Roman statues and he moved to the more informal, all-male class at the Royal Hibernian Academy, where students were free to come and go as they pleased—and where he was free of his sisters. The only surviving drawing from those student days is a workmanlike, but not particularly impressive, pastel profile of a boy's head.

In the midst of this rather unpromising start as an art student he had his first success as a poet. In 1885 the *Dublin University Review* published his pastoral verse drama, "The Island of Statues: An Arcadian Faery Tale— In Two Acts." Poetry now replaced art as the young man's career and would remain so, despite his constant worries about money during the next twenty years.

In addition to the first publication of Yeats's poetry, 1885 marked the beginning of his active involvement in occultism and in Irish nationalism. He founded the Dublin Hermetic Society in 1885 with his friend George Russell, who was to become a poet, mystic, painter, and agricultural cooperative organizer. The Dublin Hermetic Society invited an Indian guru, Mohini Chaterjee, to instruct them. Both Yeats and Russell became theosophists and remained permanently interested in occultism, although Yeats later turned from the sweeping mystical insights of theosophy to applied ritual magic.

Yeats's connection with Irish nationalism began that same year with his introduction to John O'Leary, a famous patriot who had returned to Ireland after a total of twenty years of imprisonment and exile. O'Leary had edited the weekly paper of the Irish Republican Brotherhood (the Fenians), who sought the armed overthrow of British rule in Ireland. He was widely respected for his proven loyalty to Irish nationalism and for his uncompromisingly high standard of decorousness, a quality that had particular appeal for Yeats. Portraits by John Butler Yeats show O'Leary's magnificent white beard and

intent face, which contributed to his impressiveness.
O'Leary had a keen enthusiasm for Irish books, songs,
and ballads, and he encouraged young writers like Yeats
to adopt Irish subjects for their writing. In 1889 Yeats
praised O'Leary for seeing, "more clearly than any one,"
that "there is no fine nationality without literature," and
"that there is no fine literature without nationality."[7] The
effect on Yeats's writing is clearly evident in collections
of his early poems. These open with a few pastoral poems,
featuring Arcadian shepherds, and then several Indian
poems, which show the influence of the Dublin Hermetic
Society. But all the subsequent poems are based directly
on Irish legends, Irish folklore, and Irish ballads and
songs. In his collected volume of 1895 Yeats named this
early section "Crossways" because, as he explained in a
note, he had "tried many pathways."[8] He later clarified
that explanation: "When I first wrote I went here and
there for my subjects as my reading led me, and preferred to all other countries Arcadia and the India of
romance, but presently I convinced myself . . . that I
should never go for the scenery of a poem to any country
but my own, and I think that I shall hold to that con-
viction to the end."[9]

Ironically, almost as soon as Yeats made that important change to Irish subject matter, he moved with
his family back to London at the end of 1886. There he
began his literary career in earnest, as a poet and sometimes a playwright, as an editor of William Blake, and,
to earn money, as a compiler of several collections of
Irish folklore and Irish fiction. He reviewed books—
usually on Irish topics—and wrote novels and short stories with Irish characters and scenes. His first short story,
"Dhoya," written in 1887, and his first novel, *John Sherman*, begun in 1888, were published together in 1891.
John Sherman and Dhoya, earned £30 in royalties, unlike
his money-losing volume of poems that had been published in 1889, *The Wanderings of Oisin and Other Poems*.

That first short story, despite its amateurishly ornate use of Irish legendary materials, drew enough favor from magazine editors to encourage Yeats to write twenty-two more of these brief stories during the next dozen years.

The most important event in Yeats's life during those early years in London, however, was personal rather than literary. In 1889 he began his frustrated courtship of Maud Gonne, a beautiful, statuesque woman who was one year younger than he. Like Yeats, she recently had become an Irish patriot under the tutelage of John O'Leary, and she shared some of Yeats's interest in occultism and spiritualism. Unlike Yeats, she was comfortably well off. She maintained a home in Paris and traveled frequently—in considerable style—to Ireland, where she pursued her fierce devotion to Irish nationalism. Yeats worshipped her. The impoverished young poet skipped lunches to save enough money to pay for cab fares when they were together. She strengthened his enthusiasm for Irish nationalism and suggested that he write nationalistic plays. One of those plays, *The Countess Cathleen* (1892), was dedicated to her, and in the first production of another, *Cathleen ni Houlihan* (1902), she acted the title role, as a personification of Ireland.

Yeats preferred to express his Irish nationalism in cultural rather than directly political ways. In the early 1890s he worked actively to organize the Irish Literary Society in London and in Ireland. Maud Gonne gave him some help in that venture, and in 1897 and 1898 she drew him into working alongside her at public meetings to protest against Irish celebrations of Queen Victoria's Diamond Jubilee and to raise money for a centenary memorial to the Irish rebel Wolfe Tone. Yeats continued to be an ardent suitor although he had to wait nine years before she allowed him a kiss on the lips. He proposed marriage to her several times during the decade, but she always refused. Her reluctance, however, was not based on sexual frigidity, for until 1898 she maintained a secret

liaison with a French journalist, Lucien Millevoye. Two
children were born of that affair, a son who died as an
infant in 1891, and a daughter, Iseult, who was born in
1894 and whom Maud Gonne raised as a "niece." Yeats's
first sexual encounter was at age thirty, in 1896, with
Olivia Shakespear, who remained a friend for forty years,
although their romance lasted less than a year and never
overturned Yeats's longing for Maud Gonne.

Yeats had been introduced to Olivia Shakespear by
her cousin, the poet Lionel Johnson, who was a close
friend of his in the early 1890s. Yeats dedicated the early
section ("Crossways") of his collected poems to his Irish
friend George Russell, who remained in Dublin and was
living in a theosophical commune near St. Stephen's
Green. The later section ("The Rose") of the collected
poems in 1895 was dedicated instead to Lionel Johnson,
whose finely honed aestheticism and elegant classical
education at Winchester and Oxford were appropriate
to the section's Latin epigraph, which translates as, "O
Thou Beauty of ancient days, yet ever new! too late I
loved Thee!"[10] Johnson's education set him well apart
from Yeats, but the two young men shared a keen dedication to poetry. In 1890 Johnson and Yeats were founding members of the Rhymers' Club, a group of London
poets who met to read and discuss their poems. There
were several Irishmen among the Rhymers (and Yeats
even claimed Johnson for the Irish on the basis of one
Irish grandmother), but as a group the Rhymers preferred aestheticism rather than nationalism. To an Irish
nationalist audience in 1892 Yeats complained that the
Rhymers had excluded all nationality from their poetry
and, instead, valued subjectivity and craftsmanship above
all else. He attacked the Rhymers for thinking that "poetry is an end to itself" and that "it has nothing to do
with thought . . . nothing to do with life, nothing to do
with anything but the music of cadence, and beauty of
phrase."[11]

The Rhymers' sophistication and their distance from fervently romantic Irish nationalism was not, however, as alien from Yeats's own aesthetic views as John O'Leary and Maud Gonne might have wished, for in that same essay he went on to say that Irish writers would do well to learn "a little" from the Rhymers—"a little of their devotion to form, a little of their hatred of the commonplace and the banal."[12] In 1893 he sounded much more like a Rhymer than like an Irish nationalist when he told a lecture audience, in Dublin, that literary inspiration "comes only to him who labours at rhythm and cadence, at form and style," and that Irish writers must learn that "from the old literatures of the world." He bluntly added, "We have hitherto been slovens."[13]

In London, Yeats continued his strong interest in occultism. At first he joined the London lodge of the Theosophical Society, headed by Madame Blavatsky, who sought to synthesize all religions and all occult systems. Then in 1890 he turned to the Hermetic Order of the Golden Dawn, a secret society that practiced ritual magic. The Golden Dawn offered instruction and initiation in a series of ten grades of occult and mystical adeptship. The first four ranks were preliminary to the "Inner Order," which began with the fifth level. The three highest degrees were unattainable except by magi who, perhaps like the legendary Solomon the Mage, Simon Magus, Christian Rosencreuz, and Comte de Saint-Germain, would possess the secrets of supernatural wisdom and who would have magically extended lifetimes. Yeats was powerfully fascinated by the possibility of becoming a magus, however remote the chance might be. He was convinced that the mind was capable of reaching far beyond the limits that materialistic rationalism sought to impose. A decade later, when he had progressed to the prestigious fifth grade, he entreated his fellow members of the Golden Dawn to pursue advancement even if the three highest degrees might be unattainable in life: "It matters nothing whether the Degrees above us are in the body or out of the body, for none the less we must tread this path and open this gate, and seek this light."[14] The Golden Dawn's rituals were based upon intricate cabalistic systems of symbolism, especially the hierarchical ten stations or sephiroth on the Tree of Life and their thirty-two interconnecting paths. An initiate's instruction included astrology, at which Yeats gained quite considerable expertise; divination using the tarot cards; visions induced by contemplation of colored geometrical shapes; and alchemical transmutation, regarded as an elaborate metaphor for freeing an adept from the dross of material existence in order to achieve spiritual perfection. Yeats was an active member of the Golden Dawn from 1890 to 1922. He reached the fifth grade of membership in 1893, took an important role in the leadership of the society at the turn of the century, and achieved the coveted sixth level of membership in 1914. In that same year his future wife, Georgie Hyde-Lees, joined the Golden Dawn.

Yeats's ambition to attain the Golden Dawn's supernatural wisdom conflicted with his poetical allegiance to the physical world. To become an occult magus he ultimately would be required to devote himself exclusively to the supernatural world and to sever any allegiance to the material world. In the Golden Dawn's cabalistic symbolism, a candidate seeks to raise himself from materialism of the "Kingdom," the lowest of the ten sephiroth in the Tree of Life. A magus ultimately would achieve a completely spiritual existence at the "Crown," the highest of the ten sephiroth, which is variously symbolized as the apex of the Tree of Life and as the motionless point at the center of the turning wheel of life. The loyalty of a magus, like that of a saint, is to the spiritual world, but a poet is necessarily linked to the material world where he finds the symbols necessary for public expression of his art. Yeats discussed this difference between a magus or saint and a poet in the following brief passage from an essay written in 1906:

If it be true that God is a circle whose centre is everywhere, the saint goes to the centre, the poet and artist to the ring where everything comes round again. The poet must not seek for what is still and fixed, for that has no life for him; and if he did, his style would become cold and monotonous, and his sense of beauty faint and sickly . . . but [he must] be content to find his pleasure in all that is for ever passing away that it may come again, in the beauty of women, in the fragile flowers of spring, in momentary heroic passion, in whatever is most fleeting, most impassioned.[15]

As a poet Yeats recognized the need for a public audience, and he avoided what he considered the obscurity of William Blake, who found his poetical images in private visions rather than in the familiar physical world. Yeats preferred to follow the example of John Keats, whose romanticism remained closer to the materials of life than did that of Blake or Shelley. But even so, Yeats's visionary and idealist interests were more closely aligned with Blake and Shelley than with Keats. Several of Yeats's poems in *The Wind among the Reeds* (1899) employ occult symbolism, but these poems are isolated exceptions to his normal practice of using symbols from ordinary life and from familiar traditions. His occult ambitions were a powerful force in his private thoughts, but he remained aware of his public role as a poet.

In August 1896 Yeats and one of his Rhymers' Club friends, Arthur Symons, toured the west of Ireland. Yeats showed him the Sligo landmarks that were already becoming famous through poems such as "The Lake Isle of Innisfree" (1890). Their excursion also included County Galway, which would soon be as important as Sligo in Yeats's life and art. Yeats and Symons visited the County

Galway estate of Edward Martyn, who took them to call
on a neighbor, Lady Augusta Gregory, at Coole Park.
Lady Gregory was a middle-aged widow who became a
playwright and a folklorist. During the remaining twenty-
six years of her life she was one of Yeats's closest friends.
Her estate included an eighteenth-century country house,
a walled garden, several small woods, and a shallow lake
that was made famous as the setting of Yeats's poem "The
Wild Swans at Coole." A few miles to the west lay the
Burren, a stark expanse of barren limestone hills stretch-
ing fifteen miles to the coast of the Atlantic Ocean.

Yeats stayed at Coole Park for several weeks in the
summer of 1897, and he returned in each of the next
twenty years. He welcomed this opportunity to write
and relax, and he particularly relished the continuing
invitation to associate with the traditions of the Irish
gentry in a country house filled with books and art that
had been collected by successive generations. Yeats recorded his fondness for Coole in several poems, and he
praised it in his diary in 1909: "Under its roof living
intellect is sweetened by old memories of its descent
from far off."[16]

Lady Gregory shared Yeats's enthusiasm for Irish
cultural nationalism, and in the summer of 1897 they
met with Edward Martyn to begin plans for the Irish
Literary Theatre, which sought to encourage an inno-
vative, native Irish drama. In 1899 they staged the first
of three annual productions in Dublin, using English
professional actors who performed Yeats's *The Countess
Cathleen*. Then in 1902 they supported a company of
Irish amateur actors who staged George Russell's Irish
legendary play *Deirdre* and Yeats's patriotic play *Cathleen ni Houlihan*, with Maud Gonne as Cathleen ni Houlihan. The success of that production led to the founding
of the Irish National Theatre Society, with Yeats as president. In 1903 the company made a brief appearance in
London, where its naturalistic acting style and very sim-

ple sets were praised by drama critics who were weary of London's usual fare of exaggerated acting style and elaborate sets. This small triumph in London encouraged a wealthy patron, Miss Annie E. F. Horniman, whom Yeats had met as a member of the Golden Dawn. She paid for the renovation of the Abbey Theatre in Dublin as a permanent home for the company and she gave them generous annual subsidies.

Their opening production at the Abbey Theatre, in December 1904, included plays by Yeats, Lady Gregory, and John M. Synge, the three directors of the National Theatre Society (which is usually called simply the Abbey Theatre company or the Abbey players). Yeats was represented that night with *On Baile's Strand,* the first of his several plays that use the ancient Irish heroic warrior Cuchulain (pronounced "Koo-*hoo*-lin" or "Koo-*hul*-in"). All six of John Synge's plays were given their first performances by the company, from *The Shadow of the Glen* in 1903 to *Deirdre of the Sorrows,* which he left unfinished at his death, in 1909, at the age of only thirty-seven. Synge's masterpiece, *The Playboy of the Western World,* with its savagely comic depiction of Irish rural life, caused noisy disturbances at its first production in 1907 at the Abbey Theatre. Yeats made strident public defenses of artistic freedom and refused to cut short the play's one-week run.

During the entire first decade of the twentieth century Yeats was extremely active in the management of the Abbey Theatre company. He chose plays, hired and fired actors and managers, and arranged tours for the company. Along with that, much of his attention as a writer turned from poetry to drama. He wrote ten plays during that decade, and the simple, direct style of dialogue needed for the stage had, in turn, a major effect on his poetry.

His collection of poems in 1899, *The Wind among the Reeds,* had been marked by a heavily elaborated style. But his poems now began to use simpler diction and conversational rhythms. This radical change in his poetic style can be traced in his first three collections during the new century, *In the Seven Woods* (1903), *The Green Helmet* [a play] *and Other Poems* (1910), and *Responsibilities* (1914). Several interesting poems in those collections even take style as their subject, for example, in "A Coat." Here Yeats derides his 1890s poetic style, saying that he had once adorned his poems with a coat "covered with embroideries / Out of old mythologies / From heel to throat." But now he announces brashly: "There's more enterprise / In walking naked."[17] He left the nineteenth century behind him and adopted instead a boldly direct, modern manner.

Yeats's poems during those first years of the century also show his frequent engagement in public controversy at the Abbey Theatre and in the campaign to build a gallery of modern art in Dublin. The lengthy titles and subtitles of some of those poems display their strong connection with specific public events: "On those that hated 'The Playboy of the Western World', 1907"; "To a Wealthy Man who promised a Second Subscription to the Dublin Municipal Gallery if it were proved the People wanted Pictures"; and "Romance in Ireland: On reading much of the correspondence against the Art Gallery" (now titled "September 1913").

The art gallery project was led by Hugh Lane, who was an art dealer and a nephew of Lady Gregory. Lane persuaded the Dublin city council to support a gallery of modern art, which opened in 1908 in a vacant house that was supposed to be only a temporary site until a new building was ready. Then, after four years of frustrating delay, Lane threatened to withdraw his gift of a select group of thirty-nine pictures unless a final decision was reached about a new building. A public subscription was launched and the city promptly agreed to provide £22,000, but a protracted debate developed over the

selection of a site. Lane's patience was exhausted, and
in September 1913 he transferred the pictures to London's National Gallery. In 1915 Lane drowned when the
Lusitania was torpedoed, and the pictures became the
object of a bitter dispute between the Dublin Municipal
Gallery of Modern Art and the National Gallery in London. Yeats and Lady Gregory, whom Lane had appointed
as an executor, tirelessly wrote letters, called on politi-
cians, and made speeches—all to no avail. In 1933, after
twenty-five years at the "temporary" location, the Dublin
Municipal Gallery of Modern Art was moved to its present home in Charlemont House, Parnell Square, and
thus Lane's request for a building was satisfied at last.
The controversy over the thirty-nine pictures, however,
outlived Lane, Lady Gregory, and Yeats; a temporary
compromise to share the exhibition of the pictures was
reached only in 1959.

Yeats proved that he could be an effective, practical
man of the theater, both as an administrator of the Abbey
Theatre and as a playwright. But after a decade of writing
plays for the public stage and enduring the day-to-day
frustrations of theater business, his poetical nature reasserted itself, and in 1916 he adopted a deliberately esoteric, nonrealistic dramatic style based on Japanese Noh
plays or, to use Yeats's own term, "plays for dancers."

His nationalistic fervor, which had been strongly
encouraged by Maud Gonne, had quieted in the new
century, at least partly because of her marriage, in 1903,
to Major John MacBride, an out-of-work Irish revolutionary and exile in Paris. Then in 1916 the Easter Rising,
an unsuccessful armed rebellion in Dublin, momentously
reasserted Irish nationalism in public history and in Yeats's
life. This violent, six-day battle came as a profound surprise to most Irishmen, and certainly to Yeats. He was
further stunned by the subsequent executions of the rebel
leaders, among whom was Major John MacBride.

Maud Gonne had been separated from her husband

since 1905, but his heroism in the Easter Rising and his execution by the British Army in May 1916 strengthened her already powerful dedication to the nationalist cause. Yeats was at her side in France a few weeks after MacBride's execution and once again proposed marriage to her, but took the precaution of making his offer contingent on her giving up active politics. She chose to spend her remaining thirty-seven years dressed in widow's black for an Easter Rising martyr. Yeats's twenty-seven years of rejected courtship had ended. The next summer, at age fifty-two, he proposed—unsuccessfully—to Maud Gonne's daughter, Iseult, who had just turned twenty-three. Two months later, in October 1917, he married Georgie Hyde-Lees, a twenty-five-year-old Englishwoman whom he had met in 1911. Ezra Pound was best man at the ceremony in a London registry office.

He was lucky in his marriage. "George," as she preferred to be called, was intelligent and well read, efficient in managing the household, and skilled in occultism. She was also patient enough to endure her new husband's occasional insensitivity, as when, only four days after their marriage, he wrote a poem, "Owen Aherne and his Dancers," that is filled with almost directly stated romantic longing for Iseult Gonne. That same day, whether by chance or by design, Mrs. Yeats began her "automatic writing" experiments. In this psychic phenomenon, her hand and pen could serve as unconscious instruments for the spirit world to send information to Yeats. During the next three years Yeats and his wife held some 450 sessions of automatic writing. Yeats began at once to study and organize the information they received, which by 1924 filled almost four thousand pages. The result of all this was his elaborate, systematic theories of personality and of history, which were published in *A Vision* in 1925 and then, in a substantially revised version, in 1937. Those theories, and especially a few symbolic patterns with which Yeats organized theories, provide important background to several of his later poems.

The Easter Rising had refocused Yeats's attention upon Ireland and set in motion his eventual decision to reside in Ireland rather than England. His marriage further strengthened that resolve. In an introductory verse to *Responsibilities,* his 1914 volume of poems, he asked his ancestors' pardon for not yet having married to continue his Irish lineage: "Although I have come close on forty-nine, / I have no child, I have nothing but a book." Soon after his marriage he took his bride to Ireland. They traveled to Coole, where he proudly showed her a nearby, medieval stone tower, which he named Thoor Ballylee. He had purchased the tower, together with two adjoining small cottages, for £35 from a government land board at the end of 1916. He now began a thorough renovation to prepare Thoor Ballylee as a summer residence for the family he hoped to begin. Yeats was very pleased at the birth of their daughter, Anne, in February 1919, and the new family spent the summer at Thoor Ballylee.

The Anglo-Irish War, sometimes referred to more generally as "the troubles," an increasingly ferocious series of Irish nationalist guerrilla incidents and British reprisals, prevented the Yeatses from spending the next two summers at Thoor Ballylee, especially the summer of 1921, when Mrs. Yeats was expecting a second child. Their son, Michael, was born in England in August 1921. At the end of that year England and Ireland signed a treaty giving Ireland dominion status, generally comparable to Canada or Australia. But bitter controversies erupted within the new Irish Free State over the partition of Northern Ireland and over the wording of a formal oath of allegiance to the British Crown; these led to the Irish Civil War, which lasted from June 1922 to May 1923.

In December 1921, at the signing of the treaty, Yeats

emphatically cast his lot with the new government; the opponents of the treaty included Maud Gonne. In February 1922 he bought a house in Dublin, where he took up permanent residence, after having maintained a home in England for some thirty years. He took his family to Thoor Ballylee for the spring and summer of 1922, undaunted even by rebel soldiers who blew up a stone bridge adjacent to the tower.

Yeats accepted a six-year appointment to the Senate of the Irish Free State in December 1922, at a time when rebel forces were kidnapping senators and burning their houses. Lady Gregory's family home, Roxborough, ten miles from Coole Park, was burnt to the ground by rebels in November 1922. In Dublin, Yeats's front windows were holed by one or two stray bullets, and the government posted armed sentries at his door. The poet-senator, who was at times a voracious reader of Westerns and detective novels, playfully announced that he was giving detective stories to the sentries "to train them in the highest tradition of their profession."[18]

Yeats's allegiance to aristocratic traditions was congenial to his new, public role as a senator. He regarded himself as a representative of order amid the chaotic new nation's slow progress toward stability. His public stature was further heightened by the Nobel Prize for Literature, which he won in December 1923. Yeats thoroughly enjoyed the splendid ceremony at which the Swedish monarch presented the gold Nobel medal; the honor and ceremony may well have meant more to him than the large cash prize, despite the never entirely comfortable state of his finances. Senator Yeats, now also an honorary Doctor of Letters, spent his mornings at writing and then walked along Merrion Square from his Georgian home to the Senate or to the National Gallery of Ireland, whose Board of Governors and Guardians he joined in 1924.

This was the "sixty-year-old smiling public man," the senator who, because of his interest in Irish education, made a semi-official tour of an elementary school, from which came his poem "Among School Children." Yeats's poems and plays, during his senate term and beyond, are at once local and general, personal and public, Irish and universal. At night the poet could "sweat with terror"—his phrase in the poem "Nineteen Hundred and Nineteen"—because of the violence that surrounded him during the late 1910s and early 1920s. But the poet could generalize those threatening and even horrifying local realities by linking them with the rest of the world and with all of history. The poetic energy of the poems written in response to these disturbing times gave astonishing power to his volume of poems *The Tower*, published in 1928.

Another important element of these and of his later poems was Yeats's keen awareness of old age. His romantic poems from the late 1890s often spoke of gray hair and weariness, even though those poems were written while he was still a young man. Now, when Yeats was nearly sixty, his health began to fail and he was faced with real, rather than merely imaginary, "bodily decrepitude" and nearness to death. In 1924 he learned that he had high blood pressure and was cautioned to reduce his public speaking. Doctors advised him to leave Ireland in winter, so he spent eight of his remaining fifteen winters in the Mediterranean. Prior to his final illness in January 1939, he was very seriously ill four times: October 1927 to April 1928, December 1929 to February 1930, January to February 1935, and January to March 1936. The decline of his health forced him to cut down his public activities, but he completed his full six-year term in the Senate. In a letter to Lady Gregory in 1928 he described how his last senate speech, although only three sentences long, was followed by a minute of great pain.[19]

Along with an often very keen awareness of this physical decline, Yeats's last fifteen years and the poems from those years are marked by extraordinary amounts of vitality and an appetite for life. He enjoyed presiding over a circle of young artists, poets, and playwrights in Dublin. In 1924 Yeats wrote a suitably revolutionary manifesto that was published over the names of two young Irishmen for the first of only two issues of a brash Dublin literary review, *To-Morrow*. In the same issue he printed his famous poem "Leda and the Swan," which pays close attention to the physical details of the rape of a beautiful woman by the disguised god Zeus. As an expression of gaiety in 1929 after recovering from a serious illness the year before, Yeats wrote a series of brash, vigorous poems assigned to a fictitious old peasant woman named "Crazy Jane." Her bold sexuality in these poems was designed to startle the reader, and it succeeded wonderfully. Yeats's pose as "the Wild Old Wicked Man"—the title of one of his poems from 1938—had at least some psychological basis in the favorable results of a rejuvenation operation that he underwent in 1934, at age sixty-eight. His poetical vitality was reflected in the title of his 1938 volume, *New Poems*.

In the 1930s Ireland changed in ways that Yeats disliked, sometimes intensely. His Anglo-Irish Protestant minority no longer controlled Irish society and culture. After Lady Gregory's death in 1932, the house at Coole, which now belonged to the Irish government, stood empty and desolate. Yeats had regarded the house as a symbol of traditions that he traced to the brilliant achievements of the eighteenth-century Anglo-Irish, particularly, Jonathan Swift (1667–1745). Yeats felt the need in twentieth-century Ireland for a voice as powerful as Swift's. Yeats's two other favorites among the eighteenth-century Irish were the philosopher Bishop George Berkeley (1685–1753) and the statesman Edmund Burke (1729–97). Yeats considered Berkeley "the creator of modern philosophy,"[20] for his emphasis on subjective perception. The eloquent Burke was known for his advocacy of liberal causes and then, late in his life, for his passionate opposition to the Jacobinism of the French Revolution. Yeats's preference was for the later Burke, who, in Yeats's word, had "rolled back the anarchy of the French Revolution, and perhaps saved Europe."[21] He saw these men as welcome models of great intellectual talent, independence of spirit, and a respect for traditional social forms. He regarded the graceful dignity of eighteenth-century Georgian architecture as a fit emblem for all that he admired from that period. All of this greatness stood in sharp contrast with the undistinguished commonness of contemporary society which, according to Yeats's unblushingly anti-democratic view, cared only for the interests of merchants and peasants. He did not hesitate to state his unpopular opinions, even though he became increasingly pessimistic about the possibility of reform.

His public brazenness, in the essays of *On the Boiler* (1939) and his powerful revulsion that fuels a late play, *Purgatory* (1938), are offset and enriched by the personal conflict expressed in his last poems. Yeats faced the final darkness with resolute courage that was founded partly on his vague hope for reincarnation and partly on his admiration for bold heroism in ancient Ireland and in eighteenth-century Ireland. In that heroic mood he could speak in the stern voice of his famous epitaph, which he wrote within six months of his death and which concludes his poem "Under Ben Bulben":

> Cast a cold eye
> On life, on death.
> Horseman, pass by!

But this bold sureness is complicated by the terror-struck cry at the end of another late poem, "Man and the Echo," and also by the poignantly frivolous lust for life in the last lines of the poem "Politics," which he wanted to be the closing poem in his final collection:

> But O that I were young again
> And held her in my arms.

All during his long and distinguished career Yeats was willing to face the full complexity of life. He was, from first to last, a poet whose task was to transform the local concerns of his own life by embodying them in the resonantly universal language of his poems.

2

Backgrounds for Reading Yeats's Poems

Yeats's poems are meant to be enjoyed. Their effects of sound, rhythm, or a well-turned phrase can be immediately satisfying. His poems also offer complicated resonances of meaning, found in statement, symbol, and structure. These require more sustained attention, but they offer a rich and powerful fascination for the reader.

Each of Yeats's poems offers some evidence of his fascination with sounds and words and of his masterly ability to use them. As soon as they are read aloud, the poems he wrote before 1900 display the beauty of their smoothly paced rhythms and mellifluous sounds. Following 1900, his poems also make skillful use of sound and phrase, but usually in briefer and more closely focused local effects rather than in sustained regular patterns. Often the language of these later poems is surprisingly close to ordinary speech, but distinguishes itself as poetry by astonishing invention of phrase. An example such as "slouches towards Bethlehem," the closing line of "The Second Coming," comes easily to mind.

The more complicated pleasures of his poems often require some explanation. The present chapter will introduce some background topics essential for many of the poems: the rhetorical strategy of balancing opposites when a poem confronts complex issues, Yeats's idiosyncratic theories of history and personality, his practice of arranging the contents of a volume so that the poems comment upon each other, his supple use of verse forms, and his skillful revision of poems. Then, the remaining six chapters will introduce individual poems.

The Rhetoric of Opposites

Many of Yeats's most interesting poems directly confront subjects whose complexity allows opposed, mutually exclusive views, but the poems often manage to avoid making a simplistic choice between those opposites, while maintaining an assured rhetorical confidence that allows no suggestion of confusion. In the early poem "To the Rose upon the Rood of Time," the poet expresses two ambitions that are mutually exclusive. He wants to be a poet who contributes directly to Irish life, but at the same time he desires supernatural wisdom that would isolate him from ordinary existence. Another early poem, "Fergus and the Druid," similarly focuses on the dichotomy of worldly action and mystical knowledge, of "doing" and "dreaming," which Yeats, following occult and mystical traditions, considered to be mutually exclusive. "The Old Men Admiring Themselves in the Water" mixes ugliness and beauty. "Easter, 1916" suggests that the leaders of an unsuccessful nationalist revolt were heroic martyrs and, at the same time, reckless fools. In "A Dialogue of Self and Soul" the two speakers take exactly contradictory views on the value of life.

This pattern of simultaneous opposites can be found throughout Yeats's poetry. Both sides of the dichotomy— or "antinomy," to use the term that Yeats preferred— are supported in the poem and could be true. But because these two positions are mutually contradictory, the reader assumes that they cannot be simultaneously true. Ordinarily the reader would expect to be able to discover a straightforward answer by choosing one or the other of those opposites. Their simultaneous presence in a poem, however, forces the reader to remember that to accept only one side would require ignoring the sometimes equally valid, but contradictory opposite.

The result of this complexity is not necessarily indecisiveness. For example, the leaders of the Easter Rising, who are the subjects of the poem "Easter, 1916," were genuine heroes who exerted an important influence by their devotion to Irish nationalism. They were also, however, fools for undertaking a military action that would inevitably lead to their death or imprisonment. To ignore either their heroism or their foolhardiness would be to settle for an incomplete and therefore inaccurate view of these persons. The poem, after giving evidence for both sides of an antinomy, concludes on a confident, surehanded note. Perhaps because of the usual expectation that a carefully crafted work of art will embody a coherent view of its subject, the reader is led to assume that "Easter, 1916" has achieved an insight that has resolved the antinomy, either by choosing one side or by discovering a synthesis. Instead, the poem's artistic success translates into a rhetorical success by making the reader willing to agree that the subject's complexity will thwart any hope of finding a simple answer. Artistic coherence persuades the reader to respect the simultaneously true, although mutually exclusive, opposites. The poet sees both sides of the antinomy and leads his reader to accept that inclusive, unsimplified view.

One of Yeats's interesting devices for accomplishing this is the rhetorical question, which allows him to make a statement without committing himself to a direct assertion. The interrogative form can give the impression that the statement has been left open, at least to some degree, and thus has been softened. For example, in "Easter, 1916," one of the damning assertions about the dead heroes is couched as a rhetorical question: "And what if excess of love / Bewildered them till they died?" No answer is expected or given, but the information has been voiced. And even if the poet might not know the answer to the question, a reader is likely to be persuaded that the obvious answer is: "Yes, they were bewildered." Rhetorical questions enrich and enliven many of the poems and are worthy of consideration, especially when used in conjunction with complex themes for which simultaneous, opposite views are presented.

Theories of History and Personality

Yeats's unabashedly idiosyncratic theories of history and personality, which were published in A Vision (1925, revised 1937), were formulated from information that came to him through automatic writing, a spiritualistic procedure which Mrs. Yeats and he undertook in 1917. These theories and their associated symbols captivated Yeats's imagination, and they were incorporated to some extent in many of the famous poems from the second half of his career. For a handful of less-important poems, these doctrines and symbols are the main subject.

The discussion of his theory of history in A Vision is entitled "Dove or Swan" and is aptly prefaced by his poem "Leda and the Swan," which describes the rape of Leda, a mortal woman, by the god Zeus, who has taken the shape of a swan. The dove in the title "Dove or Swan" refers to another divine visitation upon a mortal woman, when the Holy Spirit, conventionally symbolized by a dove (John 1:32) descended to the Virgin Mary (Luke 1:35 et seq.). Yeats viewed the rape of Leda and the annunciation to Mary as rare physical analogies of the mental enlightenment that a religious mystic can achieve through vision or that a magus may be able to attain with occult invocations.

Yeats also found a parallel between the children born of Leda and Mary. The rape of Leda resulted in the birth of Helen and perhaps also Clytemnestra, the two principal women in the legends of Troy. Thus, in Yeats's scheme, Leda's rape, which he arbitrarily dated at 2000 B.C., leads to the Trojan War. Because Homer took his subjects from that war, Yeats regarded it as the cornerstone of Greek civilization. Thus Yeats could claim that the achievements of classical Greece were heralded by—and perhaps even were the result of—Zeus's rape of Leda.

In Yeats's system, the Greek or pagan era lasted from 2000 B.C. to A.D. 1, when it was supplanted by the Christian era, heralded by the annunciation to Mary. Similarly, the Christian era would last for two-thousand years and then be replaced by a new civilization with pagan values that would be diametrically opposed to those of Christianity. Within these two thousand-year cycles, Yeats was fascinated by emblematic points occurring at the midpoints of the thousand-year halves of each era. At these moments of balance, a civilization could achieve special excellence, and Yeats cited as examples the splendor of Athens at 500 B.C., Byzantium at A.D. 500, and the Italian Renaissance at A.D. 1500.

In diagramming this highly schematized theory of history, Yeats employed a symbol that helped him to visualize the simultaneous presence of opposites. He compared the gradual increase or decrease of an era's power to a cone-shaped bobbin whose thread was being wound or unwound. Yeats's name for this cone was "gyre" (which he pronounced "*guy*-er").[1] He further diagrammed the interrelation of opposing values within an era by showing two interpenetrating cones or gyres. If, as illustrated in figure 1, a cross section is taken near the end of the interpenetrating cones, one cone will contribute nearly all of the area of the cross section and the other cone will contribute only a small circle at the center of cross section.

Figure 1. Interpenetrating gyres with cross sections to show
the continuously varying intermixture of opposites.

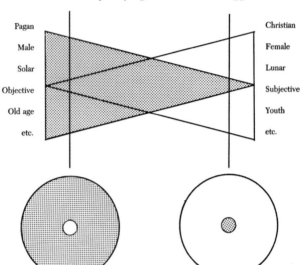

In a cross section halfway between the ends of the interpenetrating cones, the proportion from each cone will
be exactly equal. The continuously varying mixture of
the values represented by the two interpenetrating cones
gave Yeats an image for the simultaneous presence of
opposites and for continual change in the relative proportion of each. He found this representation useful for
any pair of opposites, such as pagan and Christian, male
and female, solar and lunar, objective and subjective, or
old age and youth.

Additionally, Yeats considered the cycles of history
to be analogous to the cycle of the moon's twenty-eight
phases from new moon to full moon and then back to
new moon. In *A Vision* he arranged these twenty-eight
phases around the circumference of a circle, as shown
in figure 2.

Figure 2. The Phases of the Moon.

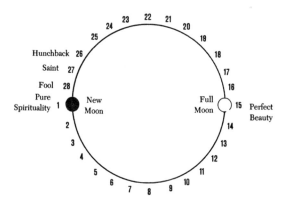

Yeats found this elaborate diagram useful for showing the relationship between opposites that face each other across the circle. He associated spirituality with the new moon (phase 1), when the moon seems to disappear from sight. Physical existence grows steadily during the first fourteen phases and reaches a maximum at the full moon (phase 15), which Yeats described as perfect beauty. In the remaining half of the cycle, physical existence gradually falls away, until it disappears completely at the new moon, where the cycle begins again. Yeats applied this pattern to an individual's life and to an historical era. The individual completes the twenty-eight phases as he advances from birth to maturity and then declines during the final phases toward death. Throughout that progression, the individual reflects a steadily changing mixture of the opposites that are represented in their unmixed, ideal form at phases 1 and 15, which are the pure spirituality of the new moon (phase 1) and the pure physicality of the full moon (phase 15). Yeats further elaborated the scheme by assigning particular phases to specific types of personality, so that although each person will pass through phases 2–14 and 16–28 during a lifetime, one phase provides an overall characterization of the individual's entire life.

"The Phases of the Moon," a poem written in 1918, carefully traces the twenty-eight phases and gives examples both of the stages in an individual life and of the personalities that are typical of each phase. In the poem, the only specific examples of persons who embody a particular phase are in phase 12, "the hero's crescent": Achilles, the legendary Greek hero at Troy, and Friedrich Nietzsche, the German philosopher who admired heroic supermen.

Many examples are available, however, in *A Vision*, where each of the twenty-eight phases receives detailed discussion. Beautiful women are in the phases adjacent to phase fifteen. Yeats considered himself a person of phase 17,[2] where the creative and intellectual powers are unusually strong. In phase 17 he could enjoy the excellent poetic company of Dante and Shelley. Shakespeare and Napoleon are in phase 20; Lady Gregory shares phase 24 with Queen Victoria. Then, just before the return to pure spirituality at phase 1, the final three phases illustrate the lessening importance of physical beauty and material accomplishments. Yeats wrote several poems about these three phases, which are characterized by the hunchback (phase 26), the saint (phase 27), and the fool (phase 28). Yeats's definition of sainthood was broad enough to allow Socrates and Pascal to occupy phase 27. Directly opposite phase 27 is phase 13, which is dominated by concern for physical beauty and is typified by the decadent artist Aubrey Beardsley.

In making these interesting (and sometimes amusing) analyses of personality, Yeats remained continually aware of the conflict between a person's interior, true self and his external mask. He first mentioned the value of masks in a simple poem written in 1910, "The Mask," where a woman reminds her lover that his interest in her depends on her mask and not on her hidden, inner self. Yeats gave eloquent expression to this idea of the mask in a group of essays, *Per Amica Silentia Lunae,* in 1917: "I think all happiness depends on the energy to assume the mask of some other life, on a re-birth as something not one's self."[3] This doctrine of the mask can be found in a wide variety of Yeats's poems. "Ego Dominus Tuus," a plainly doctrinaire poem written in 1915, praises Dante and Keats for having found the masks that enabled them to succeed as poets. At the other extreme, the doctrine of masks is amusingly applied in "Solomon and Sheba" (1918), where each of these famous characters is shown to have a contrasting inner personality behind their masks of learned king and sensuous queen.

Arrangement of Poems in a Volume

Yeats wanted his readers to think of his collected poems as a collection of individual volumes and to pay attention to the sequence of poems in each. Consequently, each of Yeats's collected editions has carefully preserved the division and arrangement of the original volumes. The opening poem in each usually establishes the dominant tone and subject. For example, "Sailing to Byzantium," at the start of *The Tower* (1928), announces the topic of old age, which appears in most of the other poems in the volume.

Smaller groups of adjacent poems often contribute to each other's meaning in more specific ways. There are narrative sequences such as "Upon a Dying Lady," a touching series of seven poems in *The Wild Swans at Coole* (1919) about the brave gaiety of Aubrey Beardsley's sister, Mabel Beardsley Wright, who lay dying of cancer. A later narrative sequence is the group of six poems beginning with "The Lady's First Song" in *New Poems* (1938), about a lady whose chambermaid acts as her surrogate in her lover's bed. Seven consecutive poems assigned to a character named Crazy Jane, in *The Winding Stair and Other Poems* (1933), enrich one another with lively glimpses of Crazy Jane's personality. That mutual strengthening of poems also operates between five consecutive poems about beggars in *Responsibilities* (1914), even without explicit narrative links between the individual works. Similarly, the juxtaposition of poems dealing with violence compounds the often horrifying power of the collection in *The Tower* (1928).

Poems are also interrelated in Yeats's volumes by verbal echoes. The richness of many of the poems in *The Wind among the Reeds* (1899) is aided by often intricate repetition between adjacent poems. This echoing of phrases in adjacent poems can be illustrated with the following two excerpts. The first pair is from the adjacent poems "He tells of a Valley full of Lovers" and "He tells of the Perfect Beauty": ". . . her *cloud-pale eyelids* falling on *dream-dimmed eyes*" is echoed by "O *cloud-pale eyelids, dream-dimmed eyes*." The second pair is from two other adjacent poems, "He bids his Beloved be at Peace" and "He reproves the Curlew": ". . . *hair* fall *over my breast*" is echoed by ". . . *hair* / That was shaken out *over my breast*" [My italics]. Three consecutive poems in *The Green Helmet and Other Poems* (1910), show similarly intricate echoing, "Peace," "Against Unworthy Praise," and "The Fascination of What's Difficult." The title of the first poem, "Peace," is repeated in the first and last lines of the next poem, which, in turn, uses the phrase "knave nor dolt" near its opening and "dolt and knave" near its ending. The third poem then also uses "knave and dolt." In *The Wild Swans at Coole* (1919), one speaker in "The People" is identified as "my phoenix," and the next poem is titled "His Phoenix." Yeats's continuing and deliberate attention to these linkings between poems can be illustrated by the fact that in 1933 he changed the title of a poem first published thirteen years earlier as "The Young Man's Song" to "Brown

Penny," adding to this sixteen-line poem's six uses of "penny," which link it to a line in the immediately preceding poem, "I had not given a *penny* for a song."[4]

Verse Forms

Another salient feature of Yeats's poetic achievement is his supple control of verse forms. He preferred the discipline of conventional stanza patterns of rhyme and line length, but he never surrendered his individual artistic freedom to manipulate metrical forms, whether in his smoothly regular early poems or in the later poems that freely use colloquial speech rhythms. For example, the enchantingly mellifluous early poem "To the Rose upon the Rood of Time" (1892) surprisingly uses heroic couplets, a verse form that is known for halting at the end of each pair of lines because of its extremely prominent rhymes. Because each pair of adjacent lines is rhymed, and because the syntax of the poem often pauses at the end of those rhymed pairs of lines, the reader usually builds a strong expectation of the second rhyme in a heroic couplet and then stops to savor the rhyme when it comes. Instead, Yeats avoided periods or other strong punctuation at the end of half of the couplets in "To the Rose upon the Rood of Time," so that the uninterrupted sentence structure keeps the reader moving, and the rhyme receives less notice. Pauses within lines also draw attention away from line endings and thus away from the rhymes. For example, the first line has two interior pauses, marked by commas: "Red Rose, proud Rose, sad Rose of all my days!" Interruptions and inversions of syntax further deemphasize rhyme. This early poem shows Yeats already able to avoid being imprisoned even by a conventional verse form as obtrusive and as "old-fashioned" as the heroic couplet, a favorite of eighteenth-century poets. In the later poems he moved away from strict metrical patterns, especially within a line, and his rhymes became much looser, although he continued to make frequent use of stanza patterns.

Revisions

Yeats enjoyed revising his poems and almost always improved them. Usually he preserved the original mood, but on a few occasions his revisions were so radical that they produced almost completely new poems. For example, few readers would suspect that the following two passages from "The Poet pleads with the Elemental Powers" are versions of the same lines. The 1894 version reads:

> And hurled it from its place amid the pearly light
> Into the blinding night,—
> O, when shall Sorrow wander no more in the land
> With Beauty hand in hand?

Its 1899 version, from *The Wind among the Reeds*, reads:

> And though the Seven Lights bowed in their dance
> and wept,
>
> The Polar Dragon slept,
> His heavy rings uncoiled from glimmering deep to
> deep:
>
> When will he wake from sleep?[5]

On another occasion he took what had been in 1890 a modestly naive, ten-line poetical portrait of an old Irishman, "The Lamentation of the Old Pensioner," and transformed it in 1925 into a hard-edged, energetic fifteen-line evocation. A comparison of a few lines from its final stanza shows the radical change: The gentle "murmur"s and the archaic "ye" of the original version's "The road-side trees keep murmuring— / Ah, wherefore murmur ye" became "There not a woman turns her face / Upon a broken tree." The final line and the refrain were even more boldly altered. The original "The well-known faces are all gone / And the fret is on me" became "I spit into the face of Time / That has transfigured me." This poem was so thoroughly changed that it would have been more suited to *The Tower* (1928), but Yeats chose to continue printing it in the 1890s section of his collected poems.

A more typical example of his mastery of revision may be seen in another early poem, "Into the Twilight." Yeats revised two of its lines three different times—in 1893, 1899, and 1902. In the original version, titled "The Celtic Twilight," published in a London magazine *The National Observer* in July 1893, these two lines read:

> Of flood and flame, or the height and wood,
> And laugh out their whimsey and work out their will.

Five months later, a revised version was published as a tailpiece to Yeats's collection of folklore anecdotes, *The Celtic Twilight*. In that first revision Yeats simply deleted "and" from the beginning of the second line. The poem's next revision, for *The Wind among the Reeds* (1899), was much more extensive and produced the version that Yeats eventually established as his favorite:

> Of sun and moon and hollow and wood
> And river and stream work out their will;

Here he abandoned the first line's veiled hint of the four elements (flood, flame, height, and wood as water, fire, air, and earth). The diction is much more direct as "flood and flame, or height"[6] is replaced by "sun and moon and hollow." Yeats strengthened the unity of tone by deleting "laugh"and "whimsey" in the second line. The replacement for them, "and river and stream," extended the smooth and long-sustained rhythm of a string of five "and"s within these two lines, as well as the visual effect of having five consecutive lines begin with "and."

Yeats again revised the poem for the second edition of *The Celtic Twilight* (1902). He exchanged the series of six, simply stated items for a more heavily elaborated series of three:

> Of hollow wood and the hilly wood
> And the changing moon work out their will.

His eight-volume collected works in 1908 grouped the 1899 version with *The Wind among the Reeds*, in volume 1, and the 1902 version with *The Celtic Twilight*, in volume 5. The 1899 version remained his choice in every subsequent printing of his poems, perhaps in part because it is more emphatic and has such a smoothly sustained pace.

Especially with the early poems, Yeats's habit of revision can sometimes require that the reader be cautious about drawing inferences, particularly about Yeats's style, before checking to find if the poem had been revised. Luckily, that task is made convenient by *The Variorum Edition of the Poems of W. B. Yeats*,[7] which gives the different published versions of Yeats's poetry.

3

~·~

The Early Poems

During his long career, Yeats made frequent and significant changes in the style of his poetry. The differences between his several poetical periods are sometimes so extreme that a reader can usefully consider the poems to have been written by different poets. In part, the changes were the result of Yeats modernizing his style as twentieth-century poetry evolved, but the shifts in his choices of poetical subjects and manner also reflected his capacity for bold transformations in his interests and attitudes during the course of his life. Thus Yeats's poetic output needs to be considered chronologically, and the remaining chapters will focus on six periods in his poetic career. Thirty-five representative poems have been selected for close scrutiny from among five hundred, and are discussed with the dual intention of tracing his career and of pointing out the values of the individual poems.

The poems are drawn from the standard collection edited by Richard J. Finneran, *The Poems: A New Edition*. This recent volume has a reliable text and arranges the poems in the order that Yeats planned, although, as in the earlier *Collected Poems of W. B. Yeats*, eight longer poems are placed in a separate "Narrative and Dramatic" section, rather than in the collections where they were first published. *The Poems: A New Edition* includes all of Yeats's own notes to the poems, as well as brief explanatory annotation. For the reader to have the poems available for convenient reference, I have listed each poem's page number in *The Poems: A New*

Edition (abbreviated: *Poems*) and in the earlier *Collected Poems of W. B. Yeats* (abbreviated: *CP*). These headings also give the dates of composition and first publication of each poem.

The Countess Kathleen and Various Legends and Lyrics (1892) (later collected in "The Rose" section)

"To the Rose upon the Rood of Time"
(1892, *Poems* 31, *CP* 31)

"To the Rose upon the Rood of Time" illustrates the lyric beauty of Yeats's early poems, and is also an important announcement of his poetic interests. Yeats himself chose this work as an introductory "program piece" at the beginning of collections of his poems from the early 1890s.

In "To the Rose upon the Rood of Time," as in most of Yeats's early poetry, the reader is carried along pleasantly by the smooth, leisurely pace and the consistently rich texture of sound. Melodious lines such as "In dancing silver-sandalled on the sea" captivated Yeats's first readers in the nineteenth century and have retained that power over succeeding generations.

This poem stands as an introduction—and almost serves as a table of contents—to poems he wrote in the early 1890s. Yeats originally published it in 1892, as the first of twenty-three poems in *The Countess Kathleen and Various Legends and Lyrics*. Subsequent collections of his poetry grouped those poems in a separate section called "The Rose," and, although Yeats often revised them and made changes in their selection and arrangement, in each of the twenty printings he kept "To the Rose upon the Rood of Time" at the start of that section as an introduction. Specifically, the second line announces that he will "sing the ancient ways," and then, as examples, mentions Cuchulain's fight with the sea and the story of Fergus and the Druid—the subjects of the two poems Yeats always placed next in "The Rose" section.

The purpose of "To the Rose upon the Rood of Time" is to announce Yeats's tasks as a poet and to show the breadth of his poetic interests, which range, even from the very beginning of his career, from private mysticism to public Irish cultural nationalism. That variety may be seen in the many uses to which "the rose" is put as a symbol in this poem. These include occult, Christian, botanical, romantic, and nationalistic references. The title alludes to the Rosicrucian rose, the emblem of a legendary occult brotherhood founded by Father Christian Rosencreuz (1378–1484). That rose is always shown at the center of a Christian cross. The back cover design for a collection of Yeats's short stories, *The Secret Rose* (1897), uses that Rosicrucian symbol. The front cover of that book is decorated with an elaborate representation of the Tree of Good and Evil, one of the Golden Dawn's most important cabalistic symbols and to which this poem refers, near the end of the first stanza, as "the boughs of love and hate." Occult emblems are left as an unobtrusive undercurrent to the poem, but they do have a role in the poem. They are allied to the Druid, to "eternal beauty," and to the poet's desire to "seek alone to hear the strange things said / By God to the bright hearts of those long dead." In opposition to spiritual "eternal beauty," the poem describes the material world of "all poor foolish things that live a day." The beautiful fragrance of the rose flower is a part of that physical world. The traditional association of red roses with romance is hinted throughout this poem, which is, after all, a personal appeal addressed to an object of beauty: the poem assigns feminine gender to "eternal beauty wandering on her way," uses carefully elevated diction ("thine own") in addressing the rose, asks beauty to "come near me," and pays her the compliment of eternal devotion (". . . red Rose of all my days").

Yeats's yearnings for Maud Gonne might echo in that address to the "proud" and "sad Rose." The beautiful Maud Gonne was certainly "proud," and she was also "sad"—about the condition of Ireland and about death, in 1891, of her infant son born of a secret affair with a French journalist. Furthermore, Maud Gonne as an ardent patriot would have relished the association of the rose with Ireland and the announcement that the poet's songs will be about "old Eire." Yeats explained, in a note at the poem's first publication: "The Rose is a favourite symbol with the Irish poets. It has given a name to more than one poem, both Gaelic and English, and is used, not merely in love poems, but in addresses to Ireland." And although Yeats said in that note, "I do not, of course, use it in this latter sense,"[1] a second note, which he added for each subsequent printing, emphasized that ever since 1887 his subject matter had been Irish.[2] The rose thus is used both as a spiritual ideal and an object of physical desire, along with its Irish backgrounds.

His particular choices of Irish subjects reflect his interest in remote, supernatural matters. He chose ancient legends rather than modern Irish subjects, and then he compounded that chronological remoteness by selecting episodes that focus on contacts with spiritual or supernatural powers rather than on feats of physical prowess. Cuchulain, the mightiest warrior among the Red Branch (Ulster) heroes, is not shown in triumphant battle or heroic love-making. Instead he is "battling with the bitter tide" because the Druids have chanted their mysteries to him for three days—as is announced in "Cuchulain's Fight with the Sea," which follows in "The Rose" section. King Conchubar (variously pronounced "*Kon*-cho-var," "*Kon*-a-chur," "*Kon*-a-har," or "*Kon*-chor")

whom the Druids serve, feared that Cuchulain's grief at
having unwittingly slain his own son might vent itself in
raging attacks upon King Conchubar's people, but the
Druids' chants delude Cuchulain into fighting against the
"invulnerable" sea. Cuchulain, a man of action, is ren-
dered ineffectual—from the perspective of ordinary life—
when his attention is shifted to magical or supernatural
things.

The opposition between ordinary and supernatural
life is clearly evident in "To the Rose upon the Rood of
Time." Ordinary life, the realm of romantic love and of
sweet "rose-breath," receives only scant attention and is
made to seem unappealing. Mortals are "blinded" by
their fate and are linked with

> . . . common things that crave;
> The weak worm hiding down in its small cave,
> The field-mouse running by me in the grass,
> And heavy mortal hopes that toil and pass.

Against those "poor foolish things that live a day" are
ranged "eternal beauty wandering on her way" and the
stars that dance "silver-sandalled on the sea" while singing "their high and lonely melody."

On this evidence it is easy to see why the poet would
shun the material world and instead invite the spiritual
Rose come near him. But to understand why the poet
would also ask that the Rose not come too close—"Ah,
leave me still / A little space"—the reader needs to recall
that the ordinary physical world is irrevocably antithetical to the ideal, spiritual realm of "eternal beauty"
where God reveals mysterious truths "to the bright hearts
of those long dead." The poet would like to discover a
compromise that would include mortal and eternal things;
he hopes to find "in all poor foolish things that live a
day, / Eternal beauty wandering on her way." He clearly
announces his attraction to the supernatural ideal, but

he also recognizes that a poet should live in the actual world. He should not "seek alone to hear the strange things said / By God" or to "learn to chaunt a tongue men do not know." The supernatural can only be pursued in isolation from ordinary life. When he speaks of seeking "alone to hear the strange things," the word "alone" can mean "only" and "in isolation from other men"; in each case the disadvantages are clear for a public poet who must write in a language his audience can understand. That struggle between spiritual and physical worlds can be seen in the next poems.

"Fergus and the Druid"
(1892, *Poems* 32, *CP* 32)

In "Fergus and the Druid," the second poem of "The Rose" section, Fergus the king abandons his worldly power so that he may gain the wisdom of the Druid. The action in the poem, like that of "Cuchulain's Fight with the Sea" (which is also mentioned in "To the Rose upon the Rood of Time"), shows that the worlds of physical action and of "dreaming wisdom" are mutually exclusive. Before Fergus abdicates his throne he tells the Druid, "A king is but a foolish labourer / Who wastes his blood to be another's dream." This opposition between action and dreaming was even more clearly stated in the original version of those lines, before a revision in 1925: "A wild and foolish labourer is a king / To do and do and do and never dream."[3] When Fergus chooses to "dream" rather than to "do," he discovers the absolute distinction between supernatural wisdom and worldly action. In a later essay, Yeats described the spiritual world as "the condition of fire," which is motionless perfection, and the physical world as "the terrestrial condition," where all power resides.[4] Because Fergus has acquired "dreaming wisdom" he has become as "nothing" in the physical world. The "little bag"—the "small slate-coloured thing"[5]—

filled with the Druid's wisdom has taught him about his prior physical incarnations, from slave to king. But Fergus's attempt to transcend ordinary life by accepting the Druid's wisdom brings unhappiness because Fergus is only partially freed from ordinary life. He is not complete magus, and he is no longer a king. He has exiled himself from the power of "doing," but he remains a mortal. Although he recognizes that each of his incarnations in ordinary life from slave to king "were wonderful and great," he now has become "nothing" because he is no longer capable of action in this world. In an early version of those lines, Fergus laments that although his new wisdom reveals to him the immortals' "eternal battle" for control of the world, he can only "feel / The pain of wounds, the labour of the spear / But have no share in loss or victory."[6] Like the Druid, whom the first stanza describes as a shape-changer who is a raven, then a weasel, and then "a thin grey man half lost in gathering night," Fergus has condemned himself to a lack of a straightforward physical identity. He is "a human shape" but is deprived of the power to act. Thus the example of Fergus should confirm the poet's earlier resolve, in "To the Rose upon the Rood of Time," not to seek "dreaming wisdom."

"The Lake Isle of Innisfree"
(1890, *Poems* 39, *CP* 39)

"The Lake Isle of Innisfree," the most popular and certainly the best known of Yeats's early poems, shares none of the supernatural concerns of "To the Rose upon the Rood of Time" or "Fergus and the Druid." The speaker of "The Lake Isle of Innisfree" seeks neither supernatural wisdom nor worldly power. Instead, the poem voices an uncomplicated desire for the pastoral calm of an imagined solitary life on a tiny, uninhabited island in Lough Gill, near Sligo. Yeats wrote the poem in 1888 while living in

London, a city that he disliked strongly at that time. The most important qualities of Innisfree, for this poem, were its beauty and isolation, as Yeats explained in a letter soon after he wrote the first draft. His choice of this particular island would also have been influenced by its nearness to Sligo, the site of his happiest memories, and perhaps also by a connection with Irish legend.[7]

The poem owes some of its popularity to the allure of pastoralism or escapism, but more than anything else, "The Lake Isle of Innisfree" works its effects through the soft, peaceful beauty of its diction, sounds, and rhythms. The overwhelmingly pastoral diction is clearly shown in the next-to-last line, where "roadway" and "pavements grey" contrast sharply with the "glade"'s and "glimmer"'s elsewhere in the poem. The rural and old-fashioned diction ("wattles," "bee-loud glade") and the old-fashioned poetic inversions of syntax ("of clay and wattles made") contribute to a mood of withdrawal and protection. The poem's pace is slowed by the additive syntactic structure and the many repetitions. There are five "and"s in the first stanza, and two lines in each of the first two stanzas begin with "and." The opening statement ("I will arise and go now") is partially repeated in that same line (". . . and go now, and go to Innisfree") and then is fully restated in the opening line of the last stanza ("I will arise and go now"). These and many other repetitions of syntax, words, and sounds help to establish a lulling, incantatory mood.

The metrical pattern of alternating lightly and heavily accented syllables is slowed in each line by the addition of an extra syllable that transforms the expected iamb (- /) into an anapest (--/) or else quietly levels the accents so that the rhythmic pattern loses its driving force. This process begins in the first line when, after a series of three iambs ("I *will* a-*rise* and *go*"), the extrametrical and lightly accented "now" intrudes to strengthen the momentary pause at the comma in the middle of the line. And exactly the same thing happens in the first line of each succeeding stanza. The regular pattern of the meter is softened further by the evenly accented last three syllables of the first stanza ("bee-loud glade") and the last three syllables of the final stanza ("deep heart's core"). This, together with the cacophonous slowness of the adjacent consonant sounds in those phrases, helps bring the poem to its resonant, motionless ending. This skillful manipulation of sounds to slow the rhythm is reinforced by the shortening of the last line of each stanza from six metrical feet to only four. And yet those short final lines in each stanza are kept firmly a part of the stanza by their strong, uncomplicated rhymes (made—glade, sings—wings, shore—core).

The Wind among the Reeds (1899)

"Into the Twilight" (1893)
"He wishes for the Cloths of Heaven"
   (1899)
(*Poems* 59, 73; *CP* 56, 70)

Yeats's mannered style and mood in the mid- and late-1890s, a period often called the "Celtic Twilight," can be illustrated with "Into the Twilight," first titled "The Celtic Twilight" (July 1893) and used as a tailpiece to a collection of prose folklore titled *The Celtic Twilight*. The luxuriant methods of this poem are applied to a colorless grey twilight setting and to a mood of exhausted retreat and of longing for a distant, even mystical, world. This short poem is intricately laced with repetitions of structure, phrase, and word. Each of the four stanzas uses the same metrical form, and the rhymes of the first stanza and the concluding phrases of its third and fourth lines are repeated in the final stanza. "Heart" is mentioned four times, the first of which is in the opening line's elaborate chiasmus: "Out-worn heart . . . time out-worn." The three other "heart"s share a syntactic pattern: "Laugh, heart, again"; "sigh, heart, again"; and "come, heart."

Another illustration of Yeats's elaborate Celtic Twilight style and also of his sometimes obscure subject matter in *The Wind among the Reeds* can be found in "He wishes for the Cloths of Heaven" (1899). In this eight-line poem there are four identical rhyme words, two of which are also used with internal rhyme: "cloths" (lines 1 and 3); "light" (lines 2, 3, and 4); "feet" (lines 5 and 7); and "dreams" (lines 6, 7, and 8). And as if that were not enough, these effects are enriched by additional internal rhymes: night—light (line 4); your—poor (lines 5, 6, and 7); and spread—tread (lines 5, 7, and 8 [twice]). The incantatory, additive syntax can be noticed in the total of five "and"s in just three lines (lines 2, 3, and 4).

But amidst all of that elaborate intricacy, which was familiar to Yeats's nineteenth-century readers, the closing lines of this poem look forward to the boldly complex rhythms he would adopt in the new century. In the final two lines, speech rhythms completely overpower the metrical pattern. A comparison of the fairly regular meter of the first two lines—"Had I the heavens' embroidered cloths, / Enwrought with golden and silver light"—with the final two lines shows that, without any sacrifice of the delicately quiet tone or without any loss of the intricate patterns of repetition, the rhythms flatten out so that the lines do not fit a metrical pattern. They slow the poem to its masterfully poignant conclusion: "I have spread my dreams under your feet; / Tread softly because you tread on my dreams."

Yeats left this poem substantially unchanged, except that its title in *The Wind among the Reeds* (1899) was "Aedh wishes for the Cloths of Heaven." Aedh is usually pronounced "Ay" (as in "hay") or "Edh." That title was part of an obscure and short-lived scheme for dramatizing many of the poems in that volume. In a mysterious note to *The Wind among the Reeds*, Yeats announced that Aedh and the other "personages" to whom half of the poems in *The Wind among the Reeds* were assigned should be thought of "more as principles of the mind than as actual personages." He added, "It is probable that only students of the magical tradition will understand me when I say . . . that Aedh, whose name is not merely the Irish form of Hugh, but the Irish for fire, is fire burning by itself."[8] One scholar has explained that Yeats was alluding to the "triplicities," an occult elaboration that expands the four elements to twelve, so that they correspond exactly with the twelve stations of the zodiac. For example, the triplicity of fire is "fire of fire," "air of fire," and "water of fire."[9] Yeats's note associated Aedh with "fire of fire," the highest member of the triplicities hierarchy. But the assignment of these poems to Aedh and two other characters, Michael Robartes and Hanrahan, was merely decorative, except insofar as the title characters lent some dramatic immediacy to their poems. The character assignments for *The Wind among the Reeds*, which Yeats did not make until February 1898, are clearly arbitrary, for almost half of Aedh's ten poems and all of Michael Robartes's three poems had been previously published either without a title persona or else assigned to Hanrahan's precursor, O'Sullivan the Red. When the poems were next published, in 1906, Yeats discarded the title attributions and never revived them.

Even so, several of the poems in *The Wind among the Reeds* contain veiled references to occult lore. Yeats himself reflected in 1908 that many of the images in these poems were "part of a mystic language, which seemed always as if it would bring me some strange revelation."[10] In "To the Rose upon the Rood of Time," a few years before *The Wind among the Reeds*, the poet makes only a hesitant and cautious invitation to the supernatural "rose." But in a poem of *The Wind among the Reeds*,

"The Secret Rose" (1896), he offers an open invitation to the "Secret Rose": "Far-off, most secret, and inviolate Rose, / Enfold me in my hour of hours." Here the hint of apocalypse ("my hour of hours") suggests that the ordinary world is finished and therefore not worthy of the speaker's continued attention or loyalty.

These occult touches did not please contemporary reviewers, one of whom complained at considerable length about Yeats's "secret avenues of thought" and "occult byways of expression":

His mysticism is sometimes mere vagueness. . . . I could wish for him that for a year or two he might neither read nor think nor hear of other mystics, and above all that the Rosicrucian cult and everything to do with esoteric mysticism might be put aside from him; and that in this interval he would set himself vigorously only to the determinable, the measurable, the attainable.[11]

If, as Yeats himself later acknowledged, much of this occult background might be thought of as "reckless obscurity,"[12] his readers could still find the rich pleasures of sound and rhythm which had delighted them in his earlier poems.

4

~~~~~~~~~~~~~~~~~~~~~~~~~~~~~~~~~~~~~~~

The New Style: 1900–1914

Yeats once reminisced that "in 1900 everybody got down off his stilts; henceforth nobody drank absinthe with his black coffee; nobody went mad; nobody committed suicide; nobody joined the Catholic church; or if they did I have forgotten."[1] The three slim volumes of Yeats's poetry published in the first fourteen years of the new century are a part of that change from the decadence of the 1890s. Those books, *In the Seven Woods* (1903), *The Green Helmet and other Poems* (1910), and *Responsibilities* (1914), display a gradual but astonishingly thoroughgoing transformation of his poetic style. At the time, many readers who had enjoyed Yeats's earlier poems were disappointed by the increasingly spare, direct manner and the present-day subject matter of these poems. More than a few of those readers concluded with regret that the poetic career of this now middle-aged Irishman had ended. During these early years of the century Yeats unquestionably spent far more of his artistic energies on drama than on poetry. Between 1903 and 1907, four of his plays were first performed or published, and he completed major revisions of two other plays. But during those five years he wrote only five lyric poems that he retained in his collected edition, and two of those lyrics were first used in short stories. The change in his poetic style reflected his new ambitions as a dramatist, for the language of plays must be simple and direct enough to be understood at one hearing by a theater audience. Many of the poems in *The Wind among the Reeds* had been almost private reveries addressed either to no one or else to partially or wholly spiritual beings. Now his poetry began to be addressed to wider audiences, with poems such as "Adam's Curse" (1903), addressed to his personal friends, and "September 1913," addressed to the Irish public.

His movement away from the richly decorated literary language and from the regular meter and rhyme of nineteenth-century poetry was both a private revolution confined to Yeats's own work and a part of a larger reformation. After 1910, Ezra Pound and others together gradually dethroned the conventional verse form of rhymed, iambic pentameter, which had been the accepted standard of English poetry for more than three hundred years.

In the Seven Woods (1903)

"Adam's Curse"
(w. 1902, publ. 1903, *Poems* 80, *CP* 78)

"Adam's Curse," which Yeats wrote in 1902, is among the earliest and most successful poems in his new manner. A new strength of diction is strikingly evident in the first stanza: "Better to go down upon your marrowbones / And scrub a kitchen pavement." He had described a closely similar labor in "The Song of the Old Mother" (1894), written less than a decade earlier and in exactly the same heroic-couplet verse form as "Adam's Curse," but with much duller, polite diction: "And then I must scrub and bake and sweep / Till stars are beginning to blink and peep."

In "Adam's Curse," he continued his practice of lessening the strong emphasis on rhyme in the heroic

couplets by trying to keep the pauses of sentence structure away from the line endings, just as in "To the Rose
upon the Rood of Time" (1892). In "Adam's Curse" only
three of the nineteen couplet rhymes are ordinary "closed"
couplets ending on a semicolon or period within a stanza
and using exact rhyme.

Rhythms show a similar increase in flexibility, notably in some daringly unmetrical, yet exquisitely poised
phrases. A striking example comes in the second line,
where the level accents of the phrase "that beautiful mild
woman" help to produce extraordinary smoothness. That
wonderfully paced phrase must have fascinated Yeats,
for in 1922 he revised the poem so as to repeat that
phrase in the second stanza: "And thereupon / That
beautiful mild woman for whose sake." This was a clear
advance over the less complex and less successful earlier
version of those lines, which had read: "That woman
then / Murmured with her young voice for whose mild
sake."

Much can be discovered about Yeats's growth as a
poet by first looking at the final two stanzas of the poem,
which have a general resemblance to his 1890s style. The
old elaborate, additive syntax is still present, for example, in the parallelism of the first two lines of the fourth
stanza ("We sat"—"We saw"). The long descriptive passage that follows is marked by the ethereal mood of his
1890s poetry:

> And in the trembling blue-green of the sky
> A moon, worn as if it had been a shell
> Washed by time's waters as they rose and fell
> About the stars and broke in days and years.

But this poem is set in actual life rather than in a scene
that could have existed only in the poet's imagination.
The moon they see in these lines is the real moon, despite
the ornate simile that describes it as "a shell / Washed

by time's waters as they rose and fell / About the stars."
In the 1890s and especially in *The Wind among the Reeds*
(1899) the reader would not have had to consider, even
momentarily, that this moon could exist in a real scene
and that the washing by time's waters is purely metaphorical.

This poem is based on an actual conversation between Yeats, Maud Gonne, and her younger sister, Mrs.
Kathleen Pilcher; it took place two or three years before
the poem was written, and Maud Gonne recorded it in
her memoirs.[2] The first three stanzas use dramatic dialogue, with a complex subtlety that moves far beyond
the poet's handling of dialogue in earlier poems such as
"Fergus and the Druid" (1892), where the reader ob-
serves the remote, legendary action of Fergus and the
Druid from afar, as though Fergus and the Druid were
actors on a stage or in a film. Those characters speak in
the present tense, and there is little direct evidence of
the poet's imagination controlling the presentation. But
"Adam's Curse," using a past-tense framework, recreates
a recent event, and one of the central intentions of the
poem is to reveal the poet's response to that dramatized
event. Three persons—two women and the poet—are
present in "Adam's Curse," but the more important of
the two women, the Maud Gonne figure to whom the
poem is addressed, does not speak. The distance from a
straightforward reenactment of a conversation is clearly
apparent in the final two stanzas, where there is no dialogue. Their dreamier style and diction are appropriate
for revealing a thought that the poet would speak only
in privacy or in a poem resulting from his imaginative
response to the actions that the earlier part of the poem
has dramatized. The poignant phrasing of the closing two
lines leaves the reader with a stunning silence that any
further dialogue or commentary would only mar.

This poem is also much more complex in its rhetorical pattern than "Fergus and the Druid." The first

three stanzas are concerned with three parallel labors that are undervalued by the present world: the poet's labor to achieve seemingly natural spontaneity, the women's labor to be beautiful, and the lovers' labor to be ceremonially courteous. The title, "Adam's Curse," is linked with these labors by the poet's statement that "there is no fine thing / Since Adam's fall but needs much labouring," for since the expulsion from the Garden of Eden, mankind has had to work. The poem describes a precious moment when their isolation from the rest of the world had allowed them to acknowledge the value of each of their labors without any explicit opposition. Beauty and romantic decorousness provide, in the final two stanzas, a temporary barrier against even the mutability that is another part of Adam's curse. This evanescent moment has been preserved in the poet's memory and has been recreated in the poem.

"The Old Men Admiring Themselves in the Water"
(w. 1902, publ. 1903, *Poems* 82, *CP* 80)

Yeats often made skillful use of titles to add a new dimension of meaning to a poem. "The Old Men Admiring Themselves in the Water," written in the same year as "Adam's Curse," is an entertaining demonstration of how a title can transform an otherwise apparently simple little poem.

If "The Old Men Admiring Themselves in the Water" is read without its title, the reader's only problem is how to accommodate the violent diction of the middle three lines of the poem:

> They had hands like claws, and their knees
> Were twisted like the old thorn-trees
> By the waters.

This central section of the poem seems ill-matched with the pair of serene three-line sentences that surround it. But the very tightly integrated rhyme scheme suggests that the serene and the violent sections are all part of one poem. The three half-lines (lines 3, 6, and 9) share a rhyme (alters—waters—waters), and the "say—away" rhyme is repeated identically in the first and last sections.

The contrast between the serenity of the old men's statement that "all that's beautiful drifts away / Like the waters" and the jarring description of them—with hands "like claws" and knees "twisted like the old thorn trees"—becomes wonderfully complicated when the reader recalls that the title of the poem announces that the grotesquely ugly old men *admire* their reflections rather than cringe in horror at them. Except for the title, the old men would simply be musing serenely, if sadly, about the inevitable loss of beauty. Their ugliness might lend a hint of melancholy, but no more. The addition of the title, however, lends an extravagant note that makes the old men seem comically absurd. They are the butts of what might seem a joke. But the dignity and truth of what the grotesque old men say can suggest that they possess a wisdom that, if the reader shared it, might permit an understanding of how they can admire themselves.

The wittiness of this poem should alert the reader to notice carefully every element in Yeats's poetry, from titles, as here, to closing refrains, especially in some later poems. The poem also illustrates the increasing modernity of Yeats's style. Although the subject matter might place the poem in the deepest recess of the "Celtic Twilight," the rhythms have turned away from regular iambic meter, here found only in the third line, and are based instead on the rhythms of speech.

The Green Helmet and Other Poems (1910)

"No Second Troy"
(w. 1908, publ. 1910, *Poems* 91, *CP* 89)

Yeats announced in "Adam's Curse" that poems should be direct and apparently simple while achieving resonant beauty. "No Second Troy" meets those high standards by combining direct biographical references—almost certainly to Maud Gonne—with the title's legendary allusion to Helen of Troy. That mixture of reality and legend is then further complicated by a fine, unresolved tension between complaints about the woman's actions and the implicit praise of her as a legendary beauty.

Maud Gonne filled the poet's days with the misery of an unrequited love from their first meeting in 1889, through the devastating shock of her marriage to Major John MacBride in 1903, and then again during the rapid failure of that marriage. Her violently anti-British attitudes and actions also match her to the poem. With Yeats often accompanying her, she spoke at rallys to raise money for the Wolfe Tone memorial of 1898; she founded the Daughters of Ireland, an Irish republican and suffragette movement at the turn of the century; and she plotted against England during the Boer War (1899–1902).

Allusions to Helen of Troy begin with the title, and continue with indirect suggestions of the woman's association with violence, high station, courage, and desire. These allusions take on a specifically ancient cast in the fine phrases that describe her "nobleness made simple as a fire" and her "beauty like a tightened bow." After the announcement that her nobleness and beauty are "not natural in an age like this, / Being high and solitary and most stern," the final line specifically refers to Troy. That echo returns the reader to the title, "No Second Troy," which, as the reader discovers, suggests the answer to the poem's final rhetorical question: "Was there another Troy for her to burn?" Her heroic qualities, though out of place in the present world, nonetheless possess a certain magnificence. But at the same time, the final word, "burn," hints at the lengthy and undeniable list of complaints about her destructiveness.

"Adam's Curse" announced that "to articulate sweet sounds together" requires considerable labor, even though that labor might not be readily apparent. "No Second Troy" illustrates the truth of that idea. The language of "No Second Troy" sounds carelessly conversational and natural. It is a simple series of four questions—a form of which Yeats will make increasingly subtle use. But no matter how casual those questions might seem, they follow a careful pattern. The two pairs of questions each begin with "Why" and "What." Each of the first two questions is five lines long; each of the second pair is one line long. Those four questions divide the twelve lines of the poem into a rhetorical structure of 5:5:1:1, superimposed on a rhyme structure that divides the poem into three equal parts, 4:4:4. Although the rhythms are so close to those of speech that the ten-syllable iambic pentameter is hardly apparent, this metrical pattern remains sufficiently powerful to make the reader elide one syllable in "ignorant" (line 3) and in "solitary" (line 10).

"The Fascination of What's Difficult"
(1910, *Poems* 93, *CP* 91)

"All Things can tempt Me"
(w. 1908, publ. 1909, *Poems* 97, *CP* 95)

The poetic craftsmanship evident in "No Second Troy" is itself the subject of several poems from this period. Yeats sometimes jotted down in prose his first ideas for a poem, and one of those that has survived is "The Fascination of What's Difficult," a poem about the craft of verse. In the following prose description, written in his

diary six months before the poem was finished, he pays
a craftsman's heed to details of rhyme and image:

Subject: To complain of the fascination of what's difficult. It
spoils spontaneity and pleasure and it wastes time. Repeat the
line ending "difficult" three times, and rhyme on bolt, exult,
colt, jolt. One could use the thought of the wild-winged and
unbroken colt [which] must drag a cart of stones out of pride
because it's difficult, and end by denouncing drama, accounts,
public contests—all that's merely difficult.[3]

The completed poem of thirteen lines has five rhymes
on "difficult" symmetrically interspersed throughout the
poem. Each of the intended rhyme words is used in the
poem, except that "exult" was replaced by "dolt." Pegasus, the winged horse emblematic of poetry, is employed exactly as described in the prose draft and with
extraordinarily vigorous language: "Shiver under the lash,
strain, sweat and jolt." And Yeats shows himself capable
of creating memorable phrases, even for expressing his
annoyance with the tiresome details of "Theatre business, management of men." Late in his life he could
claim, in the poem "What Then": "I swerved in naught, /
Something to perfection brought." His technical achievement in "The Fascination of What's Difficult" suggests
that he deserved to be confident about his skills.

The second of these poems about craftsmanship,
"All Things can tempt Me," addresses its topic in the
opening line: "All things can tempt me from this craft of
verse." Then the poem—yet another in heroic couplets—demonstrates his craftsmanship. Despite the use
of exact rhymes in all but one of the couplets (the only
imperfect rhyme is young—song), the verse form never
overpowers the poem, perhaps because lines 1, 2, and
4 all begin with a strong two-stress (spondaic) variation
from the iambic norm. The poet's command of the verse
form is strong enough to assure a reader that the extreme
variation from that iambic pattern in the final line is

deliberate. Confident of his skill, the poet speaks famil-
iarly of "this craft of verse"—"this accustomed toil" which
now comes so readily to him. As he did in "No Second
Troy," Yeats here uses biographical material, speaking
openly and even bluntly of his former distractions from
his craft: "One time it was a woman's face, or worse—/
The seeming needs of my fool-driven land."

This brief poem also proclaims the new directness
of his poetic style. He mockingly describes his former,
highly decorated style that had made much use of visions
and ancient heroic legends:

> When I was young,
> I had not given a penny for a song
> Did not the poet sing it with such airs
> That one believed he had a sword upstairs.

Now he instead seeks a plainer style, which he describes
in the final lines: "Yet would be now, could I but
have my wish, / Colder and dumber and deafer than a
fish."

Responsibilities (1914)

"A Coat"
(w. 1912, publ. 1914, *Poems* 127, *CP* 125)

"All Things can tempt Me" is the next-to-last poem in
The Green Helmet and Other Poems (1910), and at the
end of his next collection, *Responsibilities* (1914), is another ten-line poem "A Coat" whose topic again is his
new poetics.

Yeats derides his former style, maintaining that he
had once adorned his poems with a coat "covered with
embroideries / Out of old mythologies / From heel to
throat." But now, with even more brashness than the
closing line of "All Things can Tempt me," he has de-

cided: "There's more enterprise / In walking naked." This final line is the only one in the poem not to use exact rhyme; instead it has a brassily imperfect rhyme (take it—naked) particularly noticeable in these short trimeter lines.

"The Three Hermits"
(1913, *Poems* 113, *CP* 111)

Yeats's new style allowed a vigorous earthiness that he put to good use in "The Three Hermits," one of five poems he wrote in 1913 and 1914 about beggars and hermits. All of these poems employ an energetic, balladlike rhythm and all of them contrast startlingly with such ballads Yeats had written in 1888 and 1889 as "The Ballad of Father O'Hart," "The Ballad of Moll Magee," and "The Ballad of the Foxhunter." He flavored those early ballads with quaint diction (". . . ye little childer, / Ye won't fling stones at me") and poetical inversions ("To stable and to kennel go").[4] On the other hand, the decidedly unpoetic diction of "The Three Hermits" ("While he'd rummaged rags and hair, / Caught and cracked his flea") would have satisfied Ezra Pound's preference for blunt, lively language. (Yeats spent several months with Pound during the winters of 1913–14, 1914–15, and 1915–16.) Where Yeats's earlier ballads had been set in traditional English ballad measure (quatrains of rhymed alternating tetrameter and trimeter lines), "The Three Hermits" uses a sprightly, seven-syllable line (truncated trochaic), which is reminiscent of Irish language verse forms.

Interestingly, the bold stylistic details of "The Three Hermits" are combined with a deftly understated general design for accomplishing the main purpose: to praise the one hermit who achieves mystical ecstasy. The scene is unromantically cold and desolate; all three hermits are ugly and old. Ironically, the first two hermits don't notice their companion, who is the most important of the three. He "sang . . . like a bird," while one of his companions was "muttering" and the other "rummaged for a flea." Just as the first two hermits ignore the important third hermit, the poem's structure adroitly relegates him to a brief, refrainlike passage that, although it is given barely four of the poem's thirty-two lines, allows a reader to recognize that the most important of the hermits is this one who, "giddy with his hundredth year, / Sang unnoticed like a bird."

"September 1913"
(1913, *Poems* 108, *CP* 106)

With "September 1913" Yeats employs his mature new style on a subject that differs radically from the remote, evanescent subjects he had favored during the 1890s. This poem is a product of his direct involvement with Irish cultural nationalism during the first two decades of the twentieth century, when much of his work sprang from public controversies about the arts in Ireland.

Yeats here openly addresses a poem to his public opponents, as is clear in the long title used at the first publication, in a Dublin newspaper on September 8, 1913: "Romance in Ireland (On reading much of the correspondence against the Art Gallery)." To further emphasize the topicality, Yeats noted the place and date at the end of the poem: "Dublin, September 7th, 1913." The title was shortened to "Romantic Ireland (September, 1913)" for an American pamphlet in April 1914, and then was abbreviated still further to its present form, "September 1913," in the Cuala Press book *Responsibilities* (May 1914).

Each new version of the title thus became increasingly vaguer about its subject—from the newspaper version's explicit specification of a public controversy, to the present version's simple date without topic or location. In the same way, as the poem moves through its four stanzas it exhibits an increasingly less-straightforward attitude toward its subject. When the poem was published in 1914 with the short title, Yeats provided an explanatory note pointing out that the poem had arisen from the public controversy over whether or not Dublin should build an art gallery to house a collection of nineteenth-century pictures that Hugh Lane offered as a gift to the city. The opposition, led by the popular Catholic newspapers, aroused Yeats's indignation and he boldly voiced his opinion.[5] In the remaining quarter-century of his life that would become a habit, as he explained in a letter in 1936: "We may, and sometimes must be indignant and speak it. . . . Indignation is a kind of joy."[6]

That indignation, so powerfully expressed in "September 1913," grew from Yeats's perception that the opposition to the art gallery exemplified the weakening of Irish culture under the new dominance of the Catholic middle class. In his 1914 note, Yeats said that in Ireland "neither religion nor politics can of itself create minds with enough receptivity to become wise, or just or generous enough to make a nation." The note continues, "Against all this we have but a few educated men and the remnants of an old traditional culture among the poor. Both were stronger forty years ago, before the rise of our new middle class which made its first public display" in the 1890s during "the Parnellite split, showing how base at moments of excitement are minds without culture."[7]

"September 1913" makes its stinging wrath felt from the very start, in the virulence of such phrases as "fumble in a greasy till," "shivering prayer," and "have dried the marrow from the bone." They are reinforced by the strident speech rhythms of the opening lines, which easily overpower the metrical regularity of the rest of the poem. This ferocity, combined with the pronouns "you" and "your" that point directly at the public target, quite clearly suggests that the rhetoric is here intended as invective against an audience whom he deeply scorns; there seems to be little interest in trying to instruct them.

The highly pitched rhetoric of the third stanza, with its relentlessly insistent series of rhetorical questions— "Was it for this . . . / For this . . . / For this . . . / All that . . .?"—compares the poem's audience very unfavorably with the "Romantic Ireland" of John O'Leary, a nationalist hero who had died in 1907 at sixty-seven years of age, and whose fervent but decorous patriotism Yeats had much admired. O'Leary is part of the long romantic tradition of Irish nationalism and heroism. The poem mentions "the wild geese," those Irishmen who exiled themselves rather than endure a series of oppressive laws instituted between 1695 and 1727 by the English. Some of "the wild geese" volunteered for service in French armies at war with England. And the poem links O'Leary with Edward Fitzgerald and Wole Tone, whose deaths were related to the unsuccessful Rising of 1798, and with Robert Emmet, who was executed after leading another unsuccessful rebellion in 1803.

The recitation of the names of the Irish heroes implies admiration and gives them at least a momentary triumph. But if we examine the references to the heroic dead more closely we find a cold insistence on failure and death. The poem speaks of these romantic Irish heroes with considerable ambiguity. To understand this, the reader needs to recall Yeats's increasing dislike for the work of extreme Irish patriots, as he noted in an essay written soon after John O'Leary's death: "When O'Leary died I could not bring myself to go to his funeral, though I had been once his close fellow-worker, for I shrank from seeing about his grave so many whose Nationalism was different from anything he had taught or that I could share. He belonged . . . to the romantic conception of Irish Nationality on which Lionel Johnson

and myself founded, so far as it was founded on anything
but literature, our art and our Irish criticism. . . . That
ideal Ireland," perhaps now only "an imaginary Ireland,
in whose service I labour, will always be in many essen-
tials" O'Leary's Ireland.[8] Yeats had come to dislike the
tastelessness and shortsightedness of many contemporary Irish nationalists, and he strongly preferred
O'Leary's romantic tradition of heroic dedication to Ireland. But Yeats remained open-eyed in recognizing that
even O'Leary's idealism had led to failure.

Yeats skillfully modulates the poem so as not to
simplify his complex view of the Irish heroes, even though
his scorn for the contemporary middle-class Irish audience is quite clear. That his and the audience's views of
the heroes should coincide, even partially, produces a
poignancy that enriches the last two stanzas and raises
the poem above the level of simple invective from which
it probably originated. The refrain of the first stanza gives
high praise to the dead heroes: "Romantic Ireland's dead
and gone, / It's with O'Leary in the grave." But the poem
goes on to indict those heroes in each of the stanzas in
which they are mentioned. The second stanza includes
an only partially ironical reminder that the romantic Irish
nationalists had saved neither their country nor themselves: "And what, God help us, could they save?" The
third stanza characterizes the heroes' actions as "delirium"—an astonishing shock of diction that the reader is
forced to accept. The fourth stanza raises at least the
possibility that their romantic motives were less political
than personal, and less ideal than sexual: "You'd cry,
'Some woman's yellow hair / Has maddened every mother's son': / They weighed so lightly what they gave."

The ardent Irish patriot Maud Gonne was unhappy
with this poem, which she regarded as a libel on all Irish
patriots of the day, including herself, since she could feel
the sting of its refrain: "Romantic Ireland's dead and
gone, / It's with O'Leary in the grave." In her reminis-

cences she tried to explain Yeats's attack by saying that
he had written this only "because he had lost contact
with those who were working for Ireland's freedom."[9]
But Yeats's undercutting of the Irish nationalist heroes,
particularly in the charge of the last stanza that they were
"maddened" by "some woman's yellow hair," might even
have included an allusion to Maud Gonne and to Yeats
himself. The reference cannot be to the Irish nationalist
politician Charles Stewart Parnell and his dark-haired
mistress, Kitty O'Shea.[10] But Maud Gonne had rich golden
hair,[11] and, in 1897 and 1898, Yeats had sought to impress
her with his public campaigning for a Wolfe Tone centenary memorial. Maud Gonne herself recalled that in
the 1890s Yeats and she were John O'Leary's "two favourite disciples."[12] Furthermore, she had enjoyed a
memorable success as an amateur actress in the role of
Cathleen ni Houlihan, a personification of Ireland, in
one of Yeats's plays. Maud Gonne's performance in 1902
has been glowingly described in the memoirs of an actress who was in the cast: "How many who were there
that night will forget the Kathleen ni Houlihan of Maud
Gonne. . . . Watching her one could understand the
reputation she enjoyed as the most beautiful woman in
Ireland, the inspiration of the whole revolutionary movement."[13]

The ironies and indictments in "September 1913"
are at first directed solely at the Irish Catholic middle
class, addressed as "you." Next, in the second and third
stanzas, those ironies and indictments extend to include
the dead nationalist heroes, referred to as "they" and
thus separated from the Irish middle class and also from
the poet. But in the final stanza, the probable allusion
to Maud Gonne's hair makes the poet himself susceptible
to the same charges as the heroes and at least indirectly
aligns himself with them. And then, in a final compli-
cation, the pronoun used for the audience shifts from
"you" to "we," so that the poet now aligns himself both

with the audience and with the dead heroes. Therefore, the charges he has leveled at the audience and the charges he has leveled at the dead heroes are turned upon himself as well.

The complex attitude toward Irish nationalism reflects Yeats's dislike for some Irish patriots, his affection for O'Leary's view of Ireland, and his own involvement in Irish nationalism. The essay, written in 1907, in which Yeats spoke of O'Leary's romantic view of Ireland, continues: "All the while I worked with this idea, founding societies that became quickly or slowly everything I despised, one part of me looked on, mischievous and mocking, and the other part spoke words which were more and more unreal, as the attitude of mind became more and more strained and difficult."[14]

5

~~~~~~~~~~~~~~~~~~~~~~~~~~~~~~~~~~~~~

New Thoughts:
1915–1921

The Wild Swans at Coole (1919)

"Solomon to Sheba"
(1918, *Poems* 138, *CP* 136)

Yeats displays some of the imaginative and stylistic vigor
of his poetical maturity in "Solomon to Sheba," a poem
at once entertaining and complex. Solomon, the tenth-
century-B.C. king of Israel, is famed for his unsurpassed
wisdom. He is also known for his great wealth and, incidentally, for having had seven hundred wives and three
hundred concubines—although the biblical account
cautions that those very large numbers should be regarded as an exception to Solomon's usual wisdom (I
Kings 10–11). The Queen of Sheba, who ruled a wealthy
Arabian trading center in the spice trade, is rivaled only
by Cleopatra as an exemplar of exotic beauty and luxury.
In the Bible, the Queen of Sheba visited Solomon because of his reputation for great wisdom; she showered
him with lavish gifts that he matched with splendid gifts
for her.

"Solomon and Sheba" immediately announces its
spritely, balladlike tone with three alliterating initial "s"
sounds packed into the brief first line: "Sang Solomon
to Sheba." That opening note is echoed at the beginning
of the other two stanzas: "To Solomon sang Sheba" and
"Said Solomon to Sheba." Any readers who might have

expected the poem to emphasize Solomon's famous wisdom are taken aback by his singing and kissing in the first two lines. The poem's comic extravagance fully reveals itself when Sheba is shown to be sitting on Solomon's knees. This audacious pose for their dialogue is matched by a simile that compares this royal pair's conversation to a stray old horse confined in a pound:

> We have gone round and round
> In the narrow theme of love
> Like an old horse in a pound.

The simile is repeated at the end of each stanza, all of which end with the word "pound," which is further emphasized by rhyme. The repetitious, non-advancing "round and round" motion described in this simile is preceded by two repetitious pairs of lines:

> All day long from mid-day
> We have . . .
> All day long from shadowless noon
> We have gone round and round.

Further extravagance can be found in details of expression from each of the three stanzas. Solomon and Sheba's talk began at "shadowless" noon; instead of simply saying "immediately," Sheba prefers hyperbole: ". . before the sun had thrown / Our shadows on the ground." Solomon continues that pattern of exaggeration when he says, "There's not a man or woman / Born under the skies / Dare match . . ." and "There's not a thing but love. . . ." The poem's boldest invention, however, is to exchange the roles of Solomon and Sheba. Solomon becomes a sensualist who sings each of his statements and prefaces each of them by kissing Sheba. Likewise unexpectedly, Sheba spends more time in a lengthy discussion about love than in giving kisses to her lover, although love is the only topic on which she could discourse.

Despite the elaborate emphasis on "the narrow theme of love," the subject of the poem is not what Solomon and Sheba have said to each other in their long discourse on love. In fact, the descriptions and quoted dialogue reveal nothing of what Solomon or Sheba have said about love. The reader is told only that they spent an afternoon in fascinated talk about love, and that Solomon and Sheba seem to have exchanged their usual roles of savant and sensualist. The lively comedy of the poem reveals the unexpected secret selves behind the public masks of Solomon and Sheba. In a diary entry in 1909 that applies explicitly to Solomon and Sheba, Yeats combined his doctrine of masks with the lesson from "Adam's Curse" (1902), that love needs "much labouring" and is not an "idle trade":

It seems to me that true love is a discipline, and it needs so much wisdom that the love of Solomon and Sheba must have lasted. . . . Each divines the secret self of the other, and refusing to believe in the mere daily self, creates a mirror where the lover or the beloved sees an image to copy in daily life; for love also creates the Mask.[1]

And in addition to illustrating those Yeatsian doctrines, "Solomon to Sheba" manifests the value of opposites, for this man and woman, when together, can outmatch the wisdom of any other man or woman alone: "There's not a man or woman / Born under the skies / Dare match in learning with us two." Although the poem never reveals the content of their afternoon's talk about love, there is ample, lively testimony that opposites—of male and female and of mask and self—are necessary for solving love's intricacies.

"The Wild Swans at Coole"
(w. 1916, publ. 1917, *Poems* 131, *CP* 129)

The direct, simple language of "Solomon to Sheba" is characteristic of most of Yeats's poems written after the turn of the century. However, the tone of those poems

varies widely. "Solomon to Sheba" is audacious. On the
other hand, "The Wild Swans at Coole" is, to use a phrase
from its final stanza, "mysterious, beautiful," and meditative. In this quiet reverie about a landscape, memories
return to enrich the significance of the present scene.
"The Wild Swans at Coole" is written in the rich literary
tradition of what Meyer H. Abrams has called the "greater
romantic lyric" and of which Wordsworth's "Tintern
Abbey" is the best-known example.[2] In these romantic
landscape poems, the poet's memories illuminate, by
their contrast with the present scene, the changes that
have taken place in the landscape in the poet's life. This
rich texture is given further resonance by an awareness
that the future will inevitably bring further complica-
tions.

The scene described in the opening stanza of "The
Wild Swans at Coole" is a real landscape. The "trees"
and "woodland paths" are those of Lady Gregory's Coole
Park, which Yeats had visited each year since 1897, often
staying for many weeks at a time. A flock of swans that
traveled from lake to lake in County Galway and County
Mayo returned each autumn to Coole Lake, the half-
mile long, shallow lake near Lady Gregory's house. Yeats's
friend George Russell gave him an oil painting of perhaps
twenty white swans on Coole Lake. George Moore, another visitor to Coole Park, vividly recalled watching as
thirty-six white swans rose in flight from the still surface
of Coole Lake, amid "a great clamour of wings," and then
circled gracefully above the lake before returning.[3] When
a professor asked about the precise number of swans
mentioned in the poem, Yeats said that the fifty-nine
swans really were there.[4]

Swans, beautiful birds that mate for life, can symbolize lovers, and in a 1901 poem, "Baile and Aillinn,"
Yeats had used the Irish myth of two lovers who are
changed into swans and are linked by a gold chain. But
any traditional associations that the swans might have

with lovers would only serve to strengthen the melancholy, autumnal mood of this poem written in October 1916, two or three months after Maud Gonne refused his proposal of marriage. Yeats, a fifty-one-year-old bachelor who had pursued Maud Gonne for twenty-seven years, now was perplexed by his lack of concern (and perhaps even his relief) at her refusal. The result was a mood of intense depression on the October evening described in "The Wild Swans at Coole."[5]

That background, although helpful in building an appreciation of this poem, is not meant to reduce the mysteriousness that is vital to the effects produced by this "mysterious, beautiful" poem. The first suggestion of that mysteriousness comes in the autumn twilight setting, which evokes the approaching obscurity of night and of winter. The setting is laced with complicating oppositions: the dry paths as opposed to the lake's water, the water versus the sky, the mirrorlike stillness of the water versus the potential for overflow, and the swans drifting silently "on the still water" versus the swans suddenly mounting "upon their clamorous wings." Another source of mystery is the swans' exemption from aging. In this scene at Coole Lake, "all's changed"—except the swans, who are "unwearied still" and whose "hearts have not grown old." Even the syntax of the poem contributes to mystery, despite the relatively simple, often monosyllabic diction. Clarity of syntax is sacrificed to accommodate the long-sustained rhythms of sentences that are stretched to full stanza length and include long interruptions between subject and verb, as in "I" (line 15) . . . "trod" (line 18).

One useful approach for understanding the poem can be to map out its shifts between present and past. But the reader should not expect to discover a simple, linear plan, for the poem was first published with what is now its final stanza placed between the second and third stanzas. The original order of stanzas was 1–2–5–

3–4. That first version had the advantage of ending the poem on the word "still." This word's ambiguity in meaning either "motionless" or "continuing" resonates throughout the poem: "a still sky," "unwearied still," "Attend upon them still," and "the still water." But the rearrangement of stanzas into their present order enables the important statement, "All's changed," to be a fulcrum point at the center of the poem and allows the poem to end with a look to the future.

The intricate chronology of "The Wild Swans at Coole" opens with the present and then shifts to the past after the first line of the second stanza. The first line of the central stanza concludes the past tense section and is followed by two lines in the present. Then, at the center of the poem, attention shifts back to the past for the remainder of the stanza. The fourth stanza and the opening two lines of the final stanza are in the present—but here the present is equivalent to the past because the mysteriously unchanging swans are "still" as they were in the past. Then the final four lines wonder about the future.

The mysteriousness of the scene engulfs the poet, who had begun by announcing, with scientific precision, that exactly fifty-nine swans are now on the lake. In each of precisely nineteen autumns he counted or—as he reveals next—tried to count the swans, for in the first of those autumns the swans scattered in flight before he finished his count. And the sudden flight that disrupted his count is what now so powerfully dominates his memory. This quickly dissolves whatever confidence might be inspired by the mathematical precision of his accounting of the swans and autumns. Logical certainty is further eroded by the discovery that the assertion "all's changed" is not fully valid, for the swans are unchanged. Then, after the poem has so carefully established the swans' mysterious exemption from change, the final four lines inject more uncertainty: When will the swans fly away and to where will they fly? The poet's preoccupation with the flight of these at least poetically immutable swans is not a new topic, for their sudden flight was mentioned at his first attempt to count them. And even in the fourth stanza, which emphasizes the swans' changelessness, he mentions that they "wander where they will." The sense of mystery receives extra emphasis here by having the swans' eventual flight take place unnoticed, at night, while the poet will be asleep. On some future morning he will awaken to discover the change produced by the swans' departure, but the swans will be mysteriously unchanged, even after they have gone to some other lake.

The beauty of this "mysterious, beautiful" poem can be easily shown. The setting is in "autumn beauty" and the swans are "brilliant" and "beautiful." A spectacular flight of these swans many years ago had so elated the poet that he "trod with a lighter tread." Those words, however, are also a subtle reminder that his step has grown heavier with age since he first counted these beautiful swans, which will continue in the mysterious future to "delight men's eyes."

Michael Robartes and the Dancer (1921)

"Easter, 1916"
(w. & privately publ. 1916, publ. 1920,
   Poems 180, *CP* 177)

The melancholy mood that pervades the October evening of "The Wild Swans at Coole" in 1916 was also indirectly a consequence of the Easter Rising, a brief rebellion in Dublin that began on Easter Monday, April 24, 1916. Five days later, when the rebels surrendered, five hundred persons were dead and several blocks of Dublin stood in smoking ruins. Yeats, who in 1916 was living in London and had been for most of the previous thirty years, cultivated the appearance of ignoring World War I. But the Easter Rising was another matter. It proved to be the startling advent of violence that became a central concern in many of his poems, from "Easter, 1916" until at least the end of the 1920s and, to some extent, for the remainder of his life.

In order to understand this important poem it is necessary to have some fairly detailed information about the public events that inspired it, and the individual participants who are mentioned. The rebellion in Dublin had been planned as a diversionary action that would draw the attention of British troops until reinforcements of armed rebels from across Ireland could march into the city. But when the British blocked the arrival of twenty thousand rifles that Sir Roger Casement had secretly purchased in Germany, the rebel-army chief of staff prudently countermanded the orders for the Easter Rising. The Dublin contingent, led by Patrick Pearse and James Connolly, decided to proceed with their part of the operation even though they would face almost certain defeat. They seized the General Post Office in Sackville Street (now O'Connell Street) and, with a force of some eighteen hundred soldiers, took a handful of other buildings and streets in Dublin. Then they immediately proclaimed themselves the provisional government of Ireland.

The Rising, which came as a startling surprise to nearly everyone, drew very little support from the general public. Yeats was at the English country home of a friend, William Rothenstein, who recorded in his memoirs that Yeats was astounded and upset by the news of Easter Monday. Yeats explained to Rothenstein that the rebel leaders were "idealists" who were "unfit for practical affairs" and that these "good men, selfless but rash," were "throwing their lives away in a forlorn hope."[6] On Saturday, when the defeated rebels were led off to jail through the deserted streets, nearly all Irishmen were relieved that no more bullets would fly in Dublin streets, that shops could reopen and the trolleys resume normal service.

Martial law had been invoked and a series of courts-martial soon led to executions. Patrick Pearse and Thomas MacDonagh faced a firing squad on May 3rd, and two days later Major John MacBride, Maud Gonne's estranged husband, was shot. The fifteen executions ended on May 12th, when the trade union organizer James Connolly was shot while propped in a chair; his severe wounds from the fighting had left him unable to stand. Ninety-seven others, including Con Markiewicz, whom Yeats had known since 1894 in Sligo, were condemned to death, but their sentences were commuted to imprisonment. Another 122 Irishmen received prison terms from the courts-martial, and some two thousand suspected rebel sympathizers were interned.

During the first week of executions, Yeats, who remained in England until June 5th, mentioned both the "lunacy" and the "heroic, tragic" aspect of the rebels' action and their fate.[7] And on May 11th, just before the executions ended, he confided to Lady Gregory that the "Dublin tragedy" was to him a "great sorrow and anxiety": "I had no idea that any public event could so deeply move me—I am very despondent about the future."[8]

Maud Gonne, who was in France, avidly read the newspaper accounts that Yeats sent each day from England. She was convinced that the rebels' sacrifices would force Parliament to keep its word by implementing the Home Rule bill granting dominion status to Ireland. In a letter to Lady Gregory, Yeats reported that Maud Gonne's "main thought" was that "tragic dignity has returned to Ireland." This was before she learned of the execution of her estranged husband, John MacBride, but his death only strengthened her opinion. Yeats's own attention was less on the "tragic dignity" of the events, than on their "terrible beauty," for he announced in that same letter, "I am trying to write a poem on the men executed—'terrible beauty has been born again.' "[9] The poem mentioned in this letter of May 11, 1916 was "Easter, 1916," although he did not finish the poem until September 25th, a week after his arrival at Coole Park.

Yeats's strong reactions to the Easter Rising, expressed in the poem, can also be found in his letters to American and English friends. On May 23rd he wrote to John Quinn, a lawyer and patron in New York, that the Easter Rising and the executions were "a great grief" and that "a world seems to have been swept away."[10] When Yeats returned to London after a week's stay in Dublin in early June, he gave a fuller account of his reaction in a letter to the English poet Robert Bridges: "All my habits of thought and work are upset by this tragic Irish rebellion which has swept away friends and fellow workers. I have just returned from Dublin where of course one talks of nothing else, and now . . . I must go to a friend in Normandy who has been greatly troubled by it all."[11] His "friend in Normandy" was the newly widowed Maud Gonne who, from Yeats's point of view as a perennial suitor, was now free to marry. He spent all of July and August with her in Normandy, and sometime during that long visit he read a draft of the poem to her.[12] She thought the poem should give stronger praise to the dead heroes, but Yeats certainly must have considered the poem to be at least generally favorable to the rebels or else he would hardly have chosen to read it to her, even after she had (once again) refused his offer of marriage.

Yeats feared the impetus to violence and extremism that the executed martyrs of the Easter Rising had fostered. His concern was well founded, as can be seen from the example of his Irish friend George Russell, who was usually a very peaceful man. Russell, like many other Irish poets, was powerfully touched by the executions. Before and after the Easter Rising, Russell opposed the

rebels' militant version of Irish nationalism, but he offered them tribute for the profound change they effected.
Russell's poem, "Salutation," opens with qualified, but
nonetheless enthusiastic praise:

> Their dream had left me numb and cold,
> But yet my spirit rose in pride,
> Refashioning in burnished gold
> The images of those who died
> Or were shut in the penal cell.
> Here's to you, Pearse, your dream not mine,
> But yet the thought for this you fell
> Has turned life's waters into wine.[13]

Russell's poem continues with individual stanzas addressed to Pearse, MacDonagh, Connolly, and Con Markiewicz—each of whom is addressed in Yeats's poem—
and concludes with a rousing statement of the hope that
he shares with them for Irish independence.

Russell, like Yeats, was sensitive to the highly charged
political feelings in Ireland, both for and against the Easter
Rising. Both Russell and Yeats withheld their poems
from general publication, but each allowed his poem to
appear in a series of pamphlet editions of only twenty-
five copies that Clement Shorter, an English magazine
editor, printed as a hobby and gave to his friends. Shorter's wife, Dora Sigerson Shorter, was a fervent Irish
nationalist poet who was overwhelmed with grief for the
rebels' sacrifice. Her fiery poems on the Rising were also
printed in these pamphlet editions. Yeats excluded
"Easter, 1916" from his next collection of poems, *The
Wild Swans at Coole* (1917 and 1919). He did not even
allow the poem to be published in a periodical until
September 1920, four full years after he had written it.

The Easter Rising, then, was an event that pro-
foundly affected Yeats and all Irishmen, an event whose
effects are not underestimated in the refrain of Yeats's
poem: "All changed, changed utterly: / A terrible beauty

is born." Yet the Easter Rising itself was a disastrous
failure. From the moment that the coordinated national
Rising had been called off, the Dublin contingent knew
that their decision to proceed meant almost certain defeat
and probably death. Their action required equal amounts
of heroic bravery and practical stupidity—as perhaps
does every heroic act. Yeats was keenly aware that the
leaders had become heroes of nearly mythic stature, despite their foolhardiness and despite the practical failure
of the Easter Rising. He packed all of those searchingly
complex reactions into a poem that exhibits the masterful
rhetorical suppleness and power that would characterize
many of his greatest poems during the remaining twenty-
three years of his life.

"Easter, 1916" could be regarded as series of contradictory but related statements, but it is instead a single, complex statement that articulates with full honesty
his reaction to the events of Easter 1916. The contra-
dictions that the poem so forthrightly and so memorably
conveys are clearly evident in its central motif of "change."
In the opening stanza, the change proclaimed by the
refrain is surely a favorable one. In the poet's Dublin
before Easter 1916, the modern rebels' "vivid faces" contrasted with the "grey" backdrop of "eighteenth-century
houses" and with the triviality of acquaintances who were
content with "a mocking tale or a gibe" and with "polite
meaningless words"—a flat, unpoetical phrase the poet
uses twice within three lines. It was a place devoid of
energy: the opening lines mention the "close of day";
the poet "lingered awhile" and sat "around the fire at
the club," confident that the appropriate costume for all
Dubliners was the jester's "motley." Any change from
that triviality would be a good one, and the larger the
change, the better. Thus the refrain's announcement,
"All changed, changed utterly: / A terrible beauty is born,"
suggests that the change is an improvement and there-

fore welcome. "Terrible" beauty here must mean "sublime" or "awesome" beauty.

But that favorable connotation for "change" is immediately overturned in the next stanza when Con Markiewicz's voice changes from "sweet" to "shrill." The modest literary achievements of Patrick Pearse and Thomas MacDonagh are then extravagantly praised, presumably so that their execution after the Easter Rising would seem a loss for Irish literature as well as an obviously unfavorable change—death—for Pearse and MacDonagh. Pearse is described as a fellow poet (who "rode our winged horse"—Pegasus) and, with similar generosity, MacDonagh ("his helper and friend") is said to have been "coming into his force" and "might have won fame in the end." MacDonagh's most recent volume of poems, in 1913, had been an improvement over his four earlier ones, but the thirty-eight-year-old MacDonagh (a year older than Pearse) was well past the age at which his death might be compared with the early death of Chatterton or of Keats. In praising MacDonagh, Yeats showed himself willing to set aside MacDonagh's objections to revisions suggested by Yeats and Synge for his nationalistic play performed at the Abbey Theatre in 1908 and also to forgive him for having satirized Yeats (as the visionary "Earl Winton–Winton de Winton") in a play performed by a rival Dublin theater company in 1912. Thus, for Con Markiewicz, Patrick Pearse, and Thomas MacDonagh—the first three persons mentioned in this stanza—change has meant loss. But the fourth example in this stanza, Major John MacBride, reverses that unfavorable connotation of change. MacBride is first described, with some truth, as having been "a drunken, vainglorious lout" who mistreated Maud Gonne: "He had done most bitter wrong / To some who are near my heart." With a past like MacBride's, as described in the poem, perhaps any change would be an improvement, and the poem does accord him a favorable change: "He too, has resigned his part / In the casual comedy" of Dublin life prior to Easter 1916. "He, too, has been changed in his turn, / Transformed utterly." Thus, in the final line of the second stanza, the transforming "terrible beauty" has unfavorable implications for Con Markiewicz, Patrick Pearse, and Thomas MacDonagh, but it has favorable connotations for Major John MacBride. And because all four persons will be accorded the ancient heroic honor of being included in the poet's song, the change can be seen as favorable to all four of them.

This mixture of favorable and unfavorable connotations of "change" is compounded in the third stanza, which is filled with exuberantly beautiful descriptions of change and movement. But instead of associating the rebels with change, their hearts are given the emblem of a stone that disturbs the vibrantly "living stream" in whose midst it sits motionless.

The poem says that the rebels had turned their hearts to stone, an uncompromisingly direct emblem of sterility. But this unwelcome penalty comes to the rebels because they held fast to a strong-willed single-mindedness of purpose, an action that might ordinarily be praiseworthy, but which the final stanza says they had continued "too long." In 1910 Yeats had used a closely parallel idea, in an essay on Ireland, when he contrasted ever-changing Nature, "who never does the same thing twice," with "the morbid persistence of minds unsettled by some fixed idea . . . like an hysterical woman who . . . because of some logical deduction from a solitary thought has turned a portion of her mind to stone."[14]

This final stanza continues with two consecutive attempts to ease the strongly negative associations of the rebels' stony-heartedness. The poet asks, or rather wonders aloud, how much longer such sacrifices must be made, but the tone of resignation and regret clearly suggests that the question is unanswerable. He then echoes his earlier allusion, in the second stanza, to the bardic task of immortalizing heroes by listing their names in a song. What follows is an attempt to lessen the finality of the dead men's fate by an implicit likening of a poet who sings the names of the dead heroes ("murmur name upon name") to a mother who "names her child / When sleep at last has come / On limbs that had run wild."

But this tentative comparison of the heroes' death to a boy's sleep at evening is then denied with the astonishing rhetorical force of three consecutive, firmly accented negatives that are reinforced by being set in a string of five alliterating "n"s and by the repetition of "night" and "no": "What is it but nightfall? / No, no, not night but death." And as if that crushingly emphatic denial were not enough, the poet goes on to ponder aloud whether their deaths might have been "needless," for despite the vociferous opposition of Ulster Unionists, the Home Rule Bill that had been signed in September 1914 was supposed to be implemented when the World War ended.

The trite, flat language of "For all that is done and said" suggests little confidence about the hope for a peaceful political settlement, but by even mentioning that possibility, the poet gives another reminder of the dead heroes' lack of practicality. The poet is content to leave that political issue unresolved, but he breaks off in a manner that emphasizes their deaths: "Enough / To know they dreamed and are dead." And then, with diction as startlingly negative as that of "delirium of the brave" in "September 1913," he asks another question that will be left unanswered and that ends with yet more emphasis on their deaths: "And what if excess of love / Bewildered them till they died?"

The poet abandons these questions and simply lists the names of the dead heroes, for the first time in the poem. Then, just as with the endings of the first and second stanzas, this final stanza closes by restating the resolutely and resonantly ambiguous refrain:

> I write it out in a verse—
> MacDonagh and MacBride
> And Connolly and Pearse
> Now and in time to be,
> Wherever green is worn,
> Are changed, changed utterly:
> A terrible beauty is born.

The bare listing of the heroes' names gives no new information to help in judging the dead heroes, but the list of names does fulfill an expectation that was raised by two earlier references to the poet's important task of singing the names of the heroes: "I number him in the song" and "our part / To murmur name upon name." That satisfied expectation, together with the confidently majestic pacing of these final lines and the presence of the refrain, all combine to give a strong sense that the poem has reached its completion.

The refrain suggests similarities among all the various changes and transformations described in the poem, but some of those changes are favorable and some are distinctly unfavorable. The only certainty is that Easter 1916 was the occasion for profound change. The poem leaves as an open question the extent to which the named rebels should be regarded as heroes who have won immortal fame or as impractical fools who are dead. The poem delivers Yeats's complex response without having to resort to the simplification (and inevitable falsification) that might have been demanded if he had tried to describe that response in straightforward, logical prose. The truthfulness he achieves in "Easter, 1916" amply justifies poetry's warrant to avoid straightforward logic.

"The Second Coming"
(w. 1919, publ. 1920, *Poems* 187, *CP* 185)

"The Second Coming" is a spectacularly successful poetical evocation of the sudden and inexorable defeat of
the present civilization by a horrifying monster. The poem's
power and sweeping scope reside in its nightmarish use
of vivid particulars that remain suggestively broad in
their application. Like "Easter, 1916," this poem began
with the poet's reaction to disturbing political events, as
is shown by the early drafts that Mrs. Yeats rescued from
a wastebasket.[15] The rejected early drafts alluded to the
overthrow of the Russian czar in 1917, to Russia having
surrendered a large portion of Eastern Europe to Germany in 1918, and to the disintegration of the rule of
law in Ireland during 1918 and 1919.[16] However, those
specific references were replaced during the poem's
composition, probably in January 1919,[17] with a much
broader vision that incorporates Yeats's theory of two-
thousand-year cycles of history. In those cycles, each
successive civilization has values that are diametrically
opposed to those of the preceding civilization, and the
onset of each new civilization is announced by the sudden
manifestation of an avatar, such as Helen of Troy or
Christ. Yeats believed that the "twenty centuries" of the
Christian era would soon be supplanted by a new pagan
era, which the people of the present era would find
utterly alien and therefore shocking.

The poem's link with Yeats's theory of history is
hinted in the opening line's "gyre" or spiral, which describes the ever-widening circling of the falcon that "cannot hear the falconer," but also suggests the cone-shaped
figure with which Yeats schematically depicted the alternating cycles of history. Yeats explained all this in a
very long note that accompanied the poem in *Michael
Robartes and the Dancer* (1921).[18] The technical language from Yeats's theory of history is much less prom-

inent here than are the many biblical references, which make the poem all the more horrifying by inverting the usual Christian meanings of "revelation," "Second Coming," and "Bethlehem." Those disorienting inversions are underscored by the flat, unconcerned manner in which terms that are appropriate to a monster ("rough beast" and "slouches") are linked with terms that are appropriate to the infant Christ ("towards Bethlehem to be born").

The ability to impart the powerful effect of a nightmare also depends, to a very considerable extent, upon the extraordinarily effective invention of phrase, and upon the employment of rhythm to reinforce meaning. Such coinings as "the blood-dimmed tide," "the ceremony of innocence is drowned," and "vexed to nightmare" are supremely effective. The poem is full of precisely chosen verbs such as "reel," which adds to the simple circling motion an element of uncontrolled and unpredictable lurching. There are rhythmic tours de force on both large and small scales. For example, a caesura in the middle of the third line causes the line itself to "fall apart": "Things fall apart; the centre cannot hold." That rhythmic pattern of commencing the stanza with two full lines followed by a broken third line is then repeated exactly in the second stanza, where it reinforces the exclamation point that lends added emphasis to a repetition of the title:

> Surely some revelation is at hand;
> Surely the Second Coming is at hand.
> The Second Coming! Hardly are those words out. . . .

The mysterious sphinx, who—like the famous Egyptian sphinx at Giza—is male, gains considerable power from the rhythms of the poem. The reader notices, for example, the ponderous cacophony and the extreme metrical irregularity that slow the rhythms in the opening description of the monster: "Troubles my sight: some-where in sands of the desert / A shape with lion body and the head of a man." A similar effect of apt slowness may be heard in the consecutive heavy accents of "its slow thighs" in the first half of line 16: "Is *mov*-ing *its slow thighs*." The success of those rhythms can be seen clearly if that phrase is compared with the following hy-pothetical revision, which is grammatically correct and is more metrically regular, but which would be much less suitable because of its swifter rhythms: "Is *slow*-ly *mov*-ing its *thighs*." Other instances of sounds that rein-force meaning are easily found, as in the harsh "d"s of "indignant desert . . . darkness drops." And in the final line, the powerfully discomfiting effect of the diction is reinforced when the strongly regular dactylic (/--) pattern in the first part of the line, "*Slou*-ches towards *Beth*-le-hem," is flattened in the final three syllables, "to be born."

"A Prayer for my Daughter"
(1919, *Poems* 188, *CP* 185)

"A Prayer for my Daughter," the next poem in *Michael Robartes and the Dancer,* was written only a few months after "The Second Coming," when Yeats's first child, Anne, was just a few weeks old. Like "The Second Com-ing," the early drafts of this poem contained a reference to the terrors of World War I. The "ceremony of inno-cence," which is grotesquely drowned in "The Second Coming," echoes importantly in "A Prayer for my Daughter": "How but in custom and in ceremony / Are innocence and beauty born?" Each poem also mentions a cradle.[19]

In "A Prayer for my Daughter," the fifty-three-year-old poet, in his tower near Coole Park, brings all his mastery of verse to the task of protecting his newborn first child from a fierce Atlantic storm, which serves as an emblem of the perils of the modern world. Three especially noteworthy features of this poem are its astonishingly deft invention of phrase; its shifts from the chaotic rhythms of the storm into the stately, assured rhythms that connote shelter; and its statement of the values that Yeats prized.

Yeats's skillful control is first evident in the leisurely repetition of lines 7 and 9, in which he deliberately slows and calms the pace with a balanced chiasmus, in which the two halves of one line are repeated by the next line, but in the reverse sequence:

> And for an hour I have walked and prayed. . . .
> I have walked and prayed for this young child an
> hour.

This unhurried intricacy stands against the storm's violent screams:

> And heard the sea-wind *scream* upon the tower,
> And under the arches of the bridge, and *scream*,
> In the elms above the flooded stream. [My italics.]

That impending horror is accelerated by the shortened lines 14 and 15, "That the future years had come, / Dancing to a frenzied drum," and is intensified by fine invention of phrase in the lines that enclose them: "in excited reverie" and "the murderous innocence of the sea."

The third stanza opens with stately, traditional phrasing that will be repeated at the beginning of the sixth and tenth stanzas. The storm-harassed mood is calmed in the first four metrical feet by the smoothly regular meter, but then the violence intrudes to reassert itself in the piling up of heavy accents in the line's remaining two syllables: "May *she* be *gran*-ted *beau*-ty *and yet not*."

Similarly, the traditional, regular meter banishes the violence from the fifth and sixth stanzas, which articulate the poet-father's prayer for his daughter. The fifth stanza opens, "In courtesy I'd have her chiefly learned," and the next stanza continues, with a deliberately archaic inversion ("may like the linnet be"): "May she become a flourishing hidden tree / That all her thoughts may like the linnet be." Later in this same stanza, with a glancing allusion to Daphne, who was saved from Apollo's amorous improprieties and maintained her pastoral existence by being metamorphosized into a laurel tree, he opens a line with the archly old-fashioned vocative "O": "O may she live like some green laurel / Rooted in one dear perpetual place." The poet's virtuosity can be heard even in single words, as when he emphasizes the hatefulness of "intellectual" by making it rhythmically jarring, with a forced elision of one of its final syllables: "An *in*-tel-*lec*-tu-al *ha*-tred *is* the *worst*."

The opening phrase of the final stanza ("And may her . . .") links to earlier portions of his prayer by the echo of "May she" at the opening of the third and sixth stanzas. The final stanza also reintroduces the "laurel tree" image of the sixth stanza and the horn of plenty, as a classical emblem of abundance (at line 32 [with Aphrodite], at line 60 [with Maud Gonne], and at line 79). Within the same final stanza the poet emphasizes "custom" and "ceremony," which are the means for protecting his daughter. "Custom" and "ceremony" each is given three times in the stanza: "Where all's accustomed, ceremonious. . . . How but in custom and in ceremony. . . . Ceremony's a name for the rich horn, / And custom for the spreading laurel tree." Amid all of these reminders of the aristocratic refinement that he prizes so highly, the opposing "arrogance and hatred"—"the wares / Peddled in the thoroughfares"—are so completely overwhelmed as to serve only as emphasis, through contrast, for the rich custom and ceremony he seeks for her.

6

~~~~~~

Poems 1922–1926

The Tower (1928)

"Sailing to Byzantium"
(w. 1926, publ. 1927, *Poems* 193, *CP* 136)

In "A Prayer for my Daughter" Yeats was concerned with physical threats from storm and warfare as well as cultural threats from the deterioration of traditional, aristocratic values. Those external threats continue to be an important concern in the poems that Yeats wrote in the mid-1920s, but his range of topics expanded to include old age and bodily decrepitude. The resulting collection of poems, *The Tower*, published in 1928, is his finest single volume, and it might also be the finest single book of poems published in the twentieth century.

Most of the poems in *The Tower* confront the problems of physical aging. "Sailing to Byzantium" seeks to evade the impermanence of the present world by escaping into a separate world of art. The poem articulates this theme by developing a set of interwoven contrasts between youth and age, physicality and spirituality, life and art, and mortal life and eternal existence. Because of the richly elaborated echoing and reechoing of contrasts the poem is at once vivid and subtle, emphatic and complex.

The opening stanza sets "old men" against "the young /

In one another's arms." This contrast of ages is emphasized both by the fecundity of the young and the inevitable demise that awaits "whatever is begotten, born,
and dies." The birds in the trees sing "sensual music"
praising the natural process of procreation, birth, and
death. But the old man who narrates the poem prefers
"monuments of unageing intellect," which the sensual
youths "neglect." "Sensual" opposes "intellect" and "begotten, born, and dies" opposes "unageing." The opening phrase of the second stanza, "an aged man,"
immediately contrasts with "unageing" in the previous
line, and the "monuments of unageing intellect" are echoed
in the "monuments" of the soul's magnificence.

Each of the four stanzas is interlaced by references
to singing: first, the birds' "song," then the soul that is
to "sing" and seek a "singing school," then the sages who
are to be the soul's "singing-masters," and finally the
birds of "hammered gold and gold enamelling" which
"sing / To the lords and ladies of Byzantium." Yeats
explained in a note to the poem that these golden "forms"
are "artificial birds that sang."[1] The natural birds in the
first stanza sing in praise only of present life—"Whatever
is begotten, born and dies." But the song of the artificial
bird on a golden bough in Byzantium encompasses all of
the past, present and future: "Of what is past, or passing,
or to come." The artificial bird in Byzantium cares
little whether something is dead or alive or not yet
born.

The preference for artifice and for isolation from
natural life can be seen in the simile that describes Byzantium's "sages standing in God's holy fire / As in the
gold mosaic of a wall." Instead of describing the sages
by comparing them to any natural thing, the sages are
likened to a work of art—"As in the gold mosaic of a
wall." In "Sailing to Byzantium" an old man explains to
those sages and to the reader that he left his former
country and has come to Byzantium because art and the

sages there are exempt from the mortality that besets every natural body.

In 1931 Yeats commented that the poem contains some of his thoughts about an old man's proper task, which is to prepare his soul for the body's death. He further explained that because "Byzantium was the centre of European civilisation and the source of its spiritual philosophy," he had chosen to "symbolise the search for the spiritual life by a journey to that city."[2] As described in *A Vision* (1925), Byzantium has special prominence as one of the rare points of balance at which "religious, aesthetic and practical life were one." In Byzantium, during the sixth century and following, mystics who had sought supernatural visions and craftsmen who worked with physical materials shared the same culture.[3] The only direct reference to Yeat's special theory of history appears in the phrase "perne in a gyre"—that is, to move in a spiraling motion around the surface of a cone. As noted in chapter 2, Yeats used a gyre or cone as an emblem of the increasing or decreasing strength of an historical era. But in this poem, as Yeats made clear in his comment linking Byzantium with the spiritual life, Byzantium is less important as a moment in the history of civilization than as a "holy city" where the old man will find "God's holy fire" to consume his mortal body and thus free his soul from "every tatter in its mortal dress."

Another element in Byzantium's attraction for Yeats in *A Vision*, and one that might well account for the reference here to "the gold mosaic of a wall," is the unusual combination of ascetic severity and material luxury found in Byzantine art. Its starkly artificial, highly stylized forms are executed with lavish, even dazzling use of gold and other colors. In *A Vision* Yeats admiringly noted the supremacy in Byzantium of ascetics who lived amidst "incredible splendour." In the same passage, Yeats explicitly compares that physical magnificence to the beauty that can be seen only in mystical visions: " . . . An incredible splendour like that which we see pass under our closed eyelids as we lie between sleep and waking, no representation of a living world but the dream of a somnambulist . . . a supernatural splendour."[4] "Sailing to Byzantium" expresses that same duality of splendor and asceticism.

The old man in "Sailing to Byzantium" seeks an escape from mortality. He has left the country of "the young / In one another's arms" and he appeals for, but has not yet gained, entry "into the artifice of eternity." He seeks the golden splendor of Byzantium, whose supernatural, permanent beauty will replace the fecund beauty enjoyed by the young in the country he has fled. Byzantium's splendid artifice is, however, a form of physical beauty rather than an immaterial, spiritual one. The existence described in the final stanza is an escape from mortality, but it is far closer to physical existence than to an exclusively spiritual existence. Its values remain overwhelmingly aesthetic rather than ascetic. The artificial bird, which sings "to keep a drowsy Emperor awake," falls somewhat short of the expectations raised earlier in the poem by phrases such as "monuments of unageing intellect" and "monuments of its own magnificence." But at least the artificial bird is less "paltry" than "an aged man" who is merely "a tattered coat upon a stick." What matters most to the old man is that the artificial bird is not "a dying animal."

Whether this particular escape from the ravages of time would win the reader's allegiance or would even win Yeat's allegiance is an open question. But there can be no doubt that "Sailing to Byzantium" succeeds brilliantly as a poem. Its considerable reputation is amply merited by inventive imagery, by masterfully interwoven phrases and by rhythmic suppleness within the regular, ten-syllable, eight-line stanzas, each of which is rhymed on only three words (*ababab*cc).

"The Tower"
(w. 1925, publ. 1927, *Poems* 194, *CP* 192)

In 1928, when Yeats placed "Sailing to Byzantium" and
"The Tower" as the first and second poems in *The Tower*
collection, he departed from his previously consistent
practice of placing the title poem first, as with *In the
Seven Woods* (1904), *The Wild Swans at Coole* (1919),
and *Michael Robartes and the Dancer* (1921). "The Tower"
was written one year before "Sailing to Byzantium," so
the chronology of composition could not have been a
factor in his decision to open the collection with "Sailing
to Byzantium." The order chosen, besides giving special
prominence to the poem, suggests a close link between
"Sailing to Byzantium" and "The Tower." The link is that
both poems address the same problem—bodily decrepitude in old age. Both poems are spoken by old men who
are preparing their souls for the body's death. The old
man of "Sailing to Byzantium" hopes for an escape from
life into an eternal artifice, but the old man of "The
Tower" discovers a completely different answer.

    "The Tower" announces that theme in a direct ques-
tion in the opening lines:

> What shall I do with this absurdity—
> O heart, O troubled heart—this caricature,
> Decrepit age that has been tied to me
> As to a dog's tail?

The poet, although beset by old age, now finds himself
better equipped to write poetry than at any earlier time
in his life. His imagination is more passionate than it has
ever been, and he yearns more keenly than ever for
beautiful sounds and sights. He must somehow reconcile
this extraordinary difference between his bodily decrepitude and his fervent imagination. His only apparent
alternative is to stop writing poetry and control his imag-

ination by limiting his attention solely to abstractions rather than physical life. The emphatic insistence on his grotesque physical condition, in the opening section, is itself evidence of his imaginative vigor. This first section of the poem does not say whether he will be content to accept the idealist philosophers' scorn of physical things, but his sprightly diction in telling the muse to "go pack" would hardly be appropriate for an abstract philosopher. Furthermore, the question in this section is not addressed to God or to a learned philosopher or even to the poet's intellect, but rather to his heart.

Similar evidence of his imagination's strength is found in section 2, where he seeks to discover answers to the problem posed in the opening section. He uses his imagination rather than his intellect, and summons "images and memories" of imaginative vigor and of physical beauty. He further demonstrates his direct, local outlook by calling up only persons who had lived in or near this specific place, Thoor Ballylee. When the poet announces that Mrs. French lived "beyond that ridge" and the beautiful young peasant girl Mary Hynes "lived somewhere upon that rocky place," he is pointing to specific places, to that particular low ridge a mile and a half to the northeast at Peterswell and to that particular rocky place a half mile to the north. In "Meditations in Time of Civil War" (1923) Yeats mentions that this ancient tower is a physical embodiment of a poetical symbol, that the tower is a place "where the symbolic rose can break in flower." The physical setting—"under the day's declining beam" and amidst the "ruin" and the "ancient trees"—helps to prepare for the powerful and emotional use of memories from the past and for the darkening at the close of section 2 ("the sun's / Under eclipse and the day blotted out") and section 3 ("When the horizon fades . . . /Among the deepening shades").

His preference for imagination rather than intellect is also apparent in the images and memories he chooses for the poem. The imagination of Mrs. French's serving-man, who "clipped an insolent farmer's ears," worked so powerfully that he enthusiastically mistook a metaphorical expression for a literal command. Similarly, the local farmers' passionate admiration for the beauty of Mary Hynes was due to a song written by the poet Anthony Raftery (1784–1834): "So great a glory did the song confer" that "certain men, being maddened by those rhymes / . . . mistook the brightness of the moon / For the prosaic light of day." Poetical imagination enjoyed a clear victory over the intellect when that song in praise of physical beauty drove "their wits astray." The theme of a powerful poetical imagination forced to coexist with bodily deterioration returns with the reminder that the poet Raftery was blind, like Homer, who has by now replaced Plato as an appropriate classical model for the speaker.

The next ghost summoned is Red Hanrahan, a character from short stories and poems that Yeats wrote in the 1890s. The poet celebrates his own imagination's ability to have created this character and, in the description of Hanrahan, again emphasizes "decrepit age":

> He stumbled, tumbled, fumbled to and fro
> And had but broken knees for hire
> And horrible splendour of desire.

Each of the figures whom the poet summons can help to demonstrate the power of imagination—even the tower's bankrupt former owner who, as the poem playfully insists, has become "fabulous" because fables have begun to replace facts about his career as he fades in local memory. The comic interjections, as when Mrs. French is described as "gifted with so fine an ear," show that the poet has a fantastical imagination and that he is far from ready to "be content with argument and deal / In abstract things."

His reluctance to quiet his imagination because of old age is strikingly evident in the question he asks of those characters:

> "Did all old men and women, rich and poor,
> Who trod upon these rocks or passed this door,
> Whether in public or in secret rage
> As I do now against old age?"

This question is left without a direct answer, but the characters' impatience, which suggests agitation and even rage rather than serenity, provides tonal reinforcement of his own rage. When all the characters except Hanrahan have left, he asks one more question of that old lecher, who knows the secrets of the grave: "Does the imagination dwell the most / Upon a woman won or a woman lost?" This question assumes that the imagination remains active after death and further that the imagination continues to dwell upon sex. He does not ask Hanrahan for information about Hell (or Heaven) and he does not ask Hanrahan about a Platonic ideal. Instead, this question about sexual desire emphasizes his allegiance to distinctly un-Platonic behavior. Furthermore, the suggestion that the imagination dwells more on "a woman lost" than on "a woman won" is based on a preference for allowing the imagination to have complete freedom instead of being limited by the memory of actual events. None of this would be appropriate to a person who could "be content with argument and deal / In abstract things."

The intricate octave stanza[5] of section 2 is modeled on a seventeenth-century poem, Abraham Cowley's "Ode on the Death of Mr. William Harvey," and is the same stanza form that Yeats used for "In Memory of Major Robert Gregory" (1918), "A Prayer for My Daughter" (1919), and "Byzantium" (1930). With section 3, the poem shifts to markedly shorter, three-stress lines that accompany a change to a new, less elaborate tone.

Now the focus narrows to himself and the legacy
that he will leave to the young men who fish the streams
on Ben Bulben, as he did in his youth. These fishermen
will inherit his bountiful, arrogant, clear-sighted pride,
which he traces back to eighteenth-century Anglo-Irish
society, and they will inherit his absolute allegiance to
life. His explicit, vigorous rejection here of Plotinus and
Plato ("I mock Plotinus' thought / And cry in Plato's
teeth") means, according to the dichotomy presented in
the opening section of the poem, that he will continue
to celebrate the poet's power of creative imagination and
of ear and eye. Instead of making his peace with God,
he has chosen to make his peace with Italian Renaissance
art and classical Greek sculpture, which celebrate mankind and the perfection of physical beauty. This buoyant,
extravagant proclamation returns at its close to the present scene at the tower. He points to a particular loophole
where the birds are building a nest with bits and pieces
of twigs, in a manner analogous to man's creative use of
bits and pieces of art, poetry, and "memories of love, /
Memories of the words of women." The poem's return
to the local scene and to his problem of physical decay
is also apparent in the frank admission that his youthful
vigor has been "broken by / This sedentary trade" of
poetry. Earlier in this section he had been able instead
to concentrate on self-flattering imaginative associations
with "the people of Burke and of Grattan," with the horn
of plenty, and with a swan who will majestically

> fix his eye
> Upon a fading gleam,
> Float out upon a long
> Last reach of glittering stream
> And there sing his last song.

The poem's final stanza remains proudly subversive
and yet at the same time is humble and deeply touching.
The Irish expression "to make my soul," which means

"to make my soul ready for an afterlife," ordinarily carries associations of penance and attention to spiritual matters. Thus, when he announces near the end of the poem, and of his life:

> Now shall I make my soul,
> Compelling it to study
> In a learned school,

the reader might well assume that Plato and Plotinus are to be the masters of that "learned school," and that he has retracted his brazen scorn of those learned philosophers some forty lines earlier. But the poet has not surrendered. The "learned school" at which he will study is that of "learned Italian things"—the only other use of the word "learned" in the poem—and of "the proud stones of Greece" and, as the last eight lines of the poem make clear, of "poet's imaginings / And memories of love, / Memories of the words of women."

The extraordinarily emphatic description that comes next—"the wreck of body / Slow decay of blood, / Testy delirium / Or dull decrepitude"—is not used as preparation for a shift of his allegiance to an abstract, neo-Platonic spiritual concerns. Instead, those physical horrors are listed here to make the reader feel the full brunt of an even "worse evil" than the wreck of his body. That worse evil will come when life has faded so far that even "the death of friends, or death / Of every brilliant eye / That made a catch in the breath" will seem only an ordinary and unperturbing part of the natural setting. This attention to the death of friends, to memories of those friends, and to the clouds and birds of the immediate physical scene again shows that the poet would not willingly "be content with argument and deal / In abstract things."

The poem had opened in "the day's declining beam." The disappearance of "the clouds of the sky / When the

horizon fades"—as is now happening with the approach
of evening—and "a bird's sleepy cry / Among the deepening shades" evoke serenity, but also dismal and un-
wanted coldness because this peacefulness will be
accompanied by the cessation of his emotional memories.
The poet's allegiance to "imagination," to "ear and eye,"
and to "memories of love," is unalterable. And, as the
final lines so movingly suggest, that allegiance is powerful
enough for him to ignore the "battered kettle" at his
heel.

"Leda and the Swan"
(w. 1923, publ. 1924, *Poems* 214, *CP* 211)

The poems of *The Tower* record many acts of violence,
and surely one of the most horrific of them is the bestial
violation of Leda. "Leda and the Swan" pays avid, even
leering attention to the explicit physical details of that
savage mythic event, and yet, for some sixty years, the
poem has fascinated rather than offended its readers—
of both sexes.

To understand how "Leda and the Swan" can arouse
fascination rather than offense, the reader needs to recall
that the rape of Leda may be considered in several ways.
On the immediate physical level it is a bizarre sexual
incident of which the reader is a poetical voyeur. More
abstractly, the rape could be an emblem of the violence
of the Irish Civil War of 1922–23; the poem is often
published with its date, 1923, perhaps to draw attention
to those troubled times. More abstractly still, in Yeats's
theory of history the rape of Leda fits into a recurring
series of annunciations.

Yeats printed "Leda and the Swan" as an introductory poem to the "Dove or Swan" section of *A Vision*,
where he discusses his cyclical theory of history. In it,
the rape of Leda fits into a series of brief but key moments
in history when god and mortal intersect. These en-

counters, which happen only once in each two-thousand-year cycle of history, produce the avatar of the next cycle. The swan is here the messenger of a pagan annunciation, just as the dove, representing the Holy Ghost, attends the Christian annunciation. For Yeats, the violence that is so prominent in "Leda and the Swan" is also part of the parallelism between Leda and the Virgin Mary, as he shows in the poem "Wisdom," which he once intended to place immediately before "Leda and the Swan." "Wisdom" mentions the Virgin Mary's "horror" and Chirst's "wild infancy." A later poem, "A Nativity" (1938), describes Mary as "terror-struck." Leda and Mary each, if only briefly, had physical contact with an immortal and therefore each resembles, to some degree, a magus or a mystic who gains access to the supernatural wisdom of God. This was another reason for Yeats's fascination with the myth of Leda.

The rape of Leda is, of course, also distanced from ordinary experience by being mythical. In nearly all the principal versions of this legend, Zeus is attracted to the mortal Leda by her great beauty and seduces her in the form of a swan. The offspring of that seduction include at least Helen of Troy. Other versions expand the list of children, first by including the immortal Pollux (Polydeuces) and then by adding his twin brother Castor and, more rarely, Clytemnestra, who became the wife of Agamemnon. In *A Vision* (1925), which includes this poem, Yeats mentioned two of Leda's eggs, from which came "Love" and "War." He also noted that an "unhatched" egg of hers was displayed as a holy relic in a Spartan temple.[6]

Most accounts of this myth describe Zeus's action in polite euphemisms such as "visited" or "seduced." But the action of the myth is sexual and shares the explicitly physical overtones of Zeus's encounter with Europa, when he took the form of a bull. It does not use the remote symbolism of a shower of gold, the form in which he seduced Danae and fathered Perseus. Yeats's focus on the physical details of the rape is therefore available in the myth, even if his decision to give them such vigorous prominence in the poem might well be evidence that he had begun rehearsing his later role as the "Wild Wicked Old Man" of a 1938 poem.

The six successive drafts of the opening line demonstrate an increasingly explicit focus on the physical violence of the rape. Yeats's first version was predominantly narrative rather than graphic:

> Now can the swooping godhead have his will.

An intermediate version concentrated on the physical action without first establishing the context:

> A swoop upon great wings and hovering still.[7]

And then the final version carries that focus on violence even further by replacing "swoop" with "sudden blow." It adds emphasis by breaking the rhythms of the first line into two halves, with an explosive opening and an immediate halt before the line continues: "A sudden blow: the great wings beating still." The poem pays careful attention to physical details of "the staggering girl"— "thighs caressed," "helpless breast," "loosening thighs" and the "shudder in the loins"—and to sexual details like the postcoital lassitude of Zeus, mentioned in the final line ("the indifferent beak could let her drop").

Even if the sexual brutality and directness of this brief poem are set aside, its diction is sufficiently violent to permit it to contribute an ample share to *The Tower*'s evocation of the Irish Civil War's savagery: "sudden blow," "staggering," "caught," "helpless," "terrified," "shudder," "broken," "burning," "dead," and "brute blood."

The technical success of this poem, with its extraordinarily skillful manipulation of language also deserves notice. A brief list of the fine effects of diction would include the pun on "still" in the first line and the startling contrast between the pleasurable sensuousness of "her thighs caressed" and the grotesque "dark webs." Rhythmic triumphs can be found in the cacophonous violence of "shudder," which is followed by a contrasting, smoothly flowing line 10, "The broken wall, the burning roof and tower," and then the majestic slowing to a full stop in midline: "And Agamemnon dead." This broken half-line and the stanza division between lines 4 and 5 only partially disguise this fourteen-line, iambic pentameter poem's near use of the Italian sonnet form.

The final question asked—"Did she put on his knowledge with his power?"—lends an aura of mystery, despite the speculation by scholars of *A Vision* who think that Leda probably had only physical contact with Zeus, and that she did not acquire any divine wisdom before the indifferent beak could let her drop. The open question gives the poem some resonance, but does not altogether set aside an overwhelming emphasis on physicality.

"Among School Children"
(w. 1926, publ. 1927, *Poems* 215, *CP* 212)

"Among School Children," like "Sailing to Byzantium" and "The Tower," again addresses the problem of old age, but treats that theme within the complexly interrelated oppositions of imagination and reality, and of youth and age. Those antinomies are reconciled in a pair of brilliantly evocative concluding images, for which this poem is so justly famous. A chestnut tree's old roots and bole are inseparable from its youngest leaf and blossom:

> O chestnut tree, great-rooted blossomer,
> Are you the leaf, the blossom or the bole?

And a dancer's identity, while he or she is dancing, cannot be separated from the dance, which itself is embodied in the dancer:

> O body swayed to music, O brightening glance,
> How can we know the dancer from the dance?

"Among School Children" achieves resolution through its many images, which are, to a large extent, both the subject and the means of the poem. The poet's imagination discovers and evokes images that progressively illuminate and complicate the contrast between the present physical reality and the powerful images in the imagination. If the reader concentrates on those contrasts and their relation to the imagination, then this very difficult poem becomes more accessible and the application of the two final images to these contrasts becomes easier to understand.

The poem opens with "a sixty-year-old smiling public man" who is visiting a classroom of young girls. The scene is based upon Yeats's tour of a well-run Irish school, St. Otteran's in Waterford, which used the modern Montessori method for teaching the youngest girls.[8] The extreme difference in age between the old man and the schoolgirls introduces the motif of contrasting opposites and the theme of youth and age.

In stanza 2 there is a sudden shift from the public, practical activity of an old man to a private dream about a moment when Maud Gonne and Yeats were probably in their twenties. Maud Gonne—who is, of course, not present in the schoolroom—had confided one of her childhood memories to him. The poem, here taking memory as its topic, emphasizes the role of imagination and of image in relation to imagination. The poet remembers that distant moment when "it seemed that our two natures blent / Into a sphere from youthful sympathy." This blending of two separate persons, one male and one female, is recalled and expressed first as the image of a sphere, and then—just as with the pair of images at the very end of the poem—the poet gives a second possible image for it, based on Plato's *Symposium*:

"Or else, to alter Plato's parable, / Into the yolk and white of the one shell."

The old man's imagination works in stanza 3 to combine the present scene, described in stanza 1, with the memory of Maud Gonne from stanza 2. He thinks, almost idly, about Maud Gonne's former similarity to the schoolgirls. And then, suddenly, his imagination takes fire: "My heart is driven wild: / She stands before me as a living child." The image of a schoolgirl is equated with a past image of Maud Gonne, the one transformed into the other.

The motif of present and past is further enriched, in the opening line of stanza 4, when he compares the old woman's hollow, wrinkled face with her youthful image. The imagination's role in that process is emphasized by the recourse to fifteenth-century Italian Renaissance art as an aid to thinking about the old woman's present appearance:

> Her present image floats into the mind—
> Did Quattrocento finger fashion it
> Hollow of cheek as though it drank the wind
> And took a mess of shadows for its meat?

These images of youth and age lead him to remember that when he was younger his hair was more handsome than now. His thought—that he "had pretty plumage once"—breaks off casually in midline, but nonetheless affects him, for his own image as "a sixty-year-old smiling public man" is now replaced by an "old scarecrow," a quite different, but equally true self-image.

Up to this point the poem is relatively uncomplicated, except perhaps for the allusions to a "Ledaean body," which is explained by "daughters of the swan" in stanza 5, and to "Plato's parable," which is glossed in the next line. But stanza 5 extends the commitment to the idealist notions first hinted by the reference to Plato.

After the poem had been published, Yeats felt compelled
to add a note explaining that a mysterious phrase in
stanza 5, "honey of generation," comes from the neo-
Platonist philosopher Porphyry and refers to a drug that
robs infants of their recollection of prenatal, ideal freedom.[9] This arcane explanation only compounds the difficulty of the already obscure syntax in the first half of
the stanza by drawing the reader's attention more strongly
to the three-and-a-half-lines about the "honey of generation." Those lines are a very long parenthetical remark, which the reader must set aside, at least temporarily,
in order to discover that the subject and predicate of the
sentence are "mother" in line 33, and "would think" in
line 37.

The "shape upon her lap"—either an infant on her
lap or a fetus in her womb—is a son, not a daughter.
The poem, which started with schoolgirls and images of
Maud Gonne, is now focused squarely on the male
"scarecrow," the poet himself. The youthful mother's
imagining of "her son . . . / With sixty or more winters
on its head" is a contrast between infancy and old age.
It is also a contrast between the image of what the mother
hopes her son will be in old age and the scarecrow image
of the old man given in the poem. These echo the similar
contrasts in the first four stanzas between youth and age
and between the sixty-year-old smiling public man and
the old scarecrow.

Stanza 6 gives contrasting views of four great men,
any one of whom a youthful mother surely would have
thought ample "compensation for the pang of his birth,
/ Or the uncertainty of his setting forth": Plato, Aristotle,
Alexander, and Pythagoras. But the achievements of at
least the last three of those great men are described with
offhanded levity and even ridicule. Aristotle's keen interest in the physical world is preposterously caricatured
by the detail of having Aristotle whip the bottom of his
young pupil, Alexander—"a king of kings." Pythagoras,

whose legendary golden thigh was considered a mark of
his divinity and who discovered the laws of harmony,
here offhandedly plays the music of the spheres on "a
fiddlestick."[10] The poem presents Plato, Aristotle, and
Pythagoras as great philosophers and, at the same time,
as old scarecrows. The colon that closes the lines of direct
description of those great men signals their syntactical
equation with "old clothes upon old sticks to scare a
bird." Their images both as great men *and* as scarecrows
are equally valid, and both images are available in the
mixed tone of stanza 6.

Stanza 7 turns from the youthful mother's hope for
her infant to the images of religious statues that inspire
nuns, indirectly recalling the old nun in stanza 1 and the
reference to Italian Renaissance art in stanza 4. Even
those religious images will lead to a sharp contrast between heaven's perfection and earth's reality.

The final stanza offers a consoling triumph of poetic
imagination that resolves the long series of antinomies
between youth and age and between imagination and
reality. The poem has shown that in this mortal world,
even Maud Gonne as a modern Helen of Troy—a "Ledaean body," "a daughter of the swan"—cannot escape
the hollow-cheeked grotesqueness of old age. The spectacular intellectual achievements of Plato, Aristotle, and
Pythagoras cannot halt the inevitable physical deterioration of men into "old clothes upon old sticks to scare
a bird." Only in some unearthly paradise free of Adam's
curse can "labour" escape from being work and instead
be "blossoming or dancing." The poem does not offer a
solution to those insoluble problems. But the brilliantly
simple images of the chestnut tree and of the dancer
show that the antinomies are natural and that they need
not be debilitating. A chestnut tree is simultaneously
young and old; a dance, an unaging work of art, is inseparable from a mortal dancer. The poem thus removes
at least the terror of strangeness from aging and mortality

by showing that they are familiar, ordinary, and integral parts of life.

The complex and fertile interplay between the immediate scene in the schoolroom and what the poet makes of it richly demonstrates the power of imagination. And although the distance between opposites cannot be overcome in life, the final images, which are products of the imagination, show that those apparent opposites are inextricably one. This triumph of the poetical imagination offers a consolation amid all the violence of *The Tower* poems.

7

~~~~~~~~~~~~~~~~~~~~~~~~~~~~~~~~~~~~~~

Poems 1927–1935

The Winding Stair and Other Poems (1933)

"A Dialogue of Self and Soul"
(w. 1927, publ. 1929, *Poems* 234, *CP* 230)

"A Dialogue of Self and Soul" returns, with a much tighter focus than "Among School Children," to the same topic Yeats had addressed in "Sailing to Byzantium" and "The Tower": physical deterioration that frustrates the still-vigorous imagination of an old man. "A Dialogue of Self and Soul," as a dramatic dialogue, has two answers to the dilemma of old age. *My Soul* advocates an escape from life, as in "Sailing to Byzantium." *My Self* prefers a full acceptance of life, as in much of "The Tower." The title suggests that the participants in this philosophical dialogue might be generalized abstractions, "Self" and "Soul." But instead the two speakers are particularized as *My Self* and *My Soul*. Furthermore, dramatic conflict between the speakers enlivens the poem as *My Self* gains a victory over *My Soul*. *My Self*, who sings the bitter-sweetness of accepting life and who chooses rebirth rather than deliverance from life, wins sufficient control over the poem to indicate that "A Dialogue of Self and Soul" rejects *My Soul*'s suggestion of escaping out of nature as a solution to the problem of aging.

Yeats made his intention for the poem clear in a letter to his friend Olivia Shakespear: "I am writing a new tower poem 'Sword and Tower,' which is a choice of rebirth rather than deliverance from birth. I make my Japanese sword and its silk covering my symbol of life."[1] Although he eventually used a different title, the sword and tower remained the two principal symbols. Yeats's tower, Thoor Ballylee, with its winding stair and crumbling battlement, had already been made famous in his 1928 collection, *The Tower*. His 550-year-old Japanese sword, which had been given to him in 1920 by a young Japanese civil servant, Junzo Sato, is used in the poem as the principal emblem of *My Self*. Every detail mentioned about the sword fits into a carefully elaborated opposition with *My Soul's* equally significant use of the tower. The wealth of emblematic detail both simplifies and enriches the poem. To avoid any confusion, the poem tells us explicitly how these details are used. *My Soul* points out that the scabbard's embroidered silk covering, which is "from some courtlady's dress," and the sword itself "are / Emblematical of love and war." *My Self* says: "All these I set / For emblems of the day against the tower / Emblematical of the night."

The elaborately paralleled opposition of soul–tower–night–escape versus self–sword–day–activity informs the poem, and along with the dialogue form keeps the main issues clear, even when the reader is faced with difficulties of elliptical syntax. One example of those syntactic hurdles is in the first stanza, when *My Soul* exhorts *My Self* to "fix every wandering thought upon / That quarter where all thought is done." The reader needs to know that "quarter" is an allusion to Yeats's system of the lunar phases and that the word "done" carries the sense of "over and done with" rather than "accomplished." As another example, the elliptical closing line of *My Self's* first stanza might seem difficult, but because of the repeated emphasis on "still" the reader can supply the omitted words: "Can, [although] tattered, still protect, [and can, although] faded [still] adorn."

The more closely the poem is examined the more details of parallels and contrasts can be found among its emblems. Tower and sword are each "ancient." The tower's "broken, crumbling battlement" is, like the sword, a device of warfare and parallels the "tattered" condition of the sword's scabbard. *My Soul*'s "breathless [a pun on "without breath"] starlit air" is opposed to life. The goal sought by *My Soul* is "hidden" as opposed to the "looking-glass" brightness and clarity of the sword blade. *My Soul* tells *My Self* to stop thinking about the things of life, but *My Self* counters by paying even more detailed attention to the sword, naming its maker, Montashigi, and then further specifying "third of his family."

My Self is "long past his prime" and "in the wintry blast"; he is as "broken, crumbling" and "tattered" as the battlement and the scabbard. But *My Self*'s imagination is, like the sword blade, "still as it was, / Still razor-keen." *My Self* rejects *My Soul*'s wish for deliverance "from the crime of death and birth" and claims instead "a charter to commit the crime once more"—to be reincarnated and to live again. *My Self* scorns *My Soul*'s statements so completely that this echoing reference to "the crime" is the only evidence that *My Self* has paid any attention to what *My Soul* has said.

At the end of section 1, *My Soul* makes his final statement. He praises the loss of hearing, speech, and sight—"man is stricken deaf and dumb and blind"—in an ascent to heaven and then, in the spiritual fullness of that thought, *My Soul* is stricken dumb—"my tongue's a stone." All of section 2, which is spoken by *My Self*, builds to the final stanza's point-by-point refutation of the argument with which *My Soul* had ended section 1.

My Self opens section 2 with a frank acknowledgment that is altogether different from the spiritual ecstasy just described by *My Soul*. *My Self* says: "A living man is blind and drinks his drop." And then *My Self* brushes aside *My Soul*'s argument by saying, "What matter if the

ditches are impure? / What matter if I live it all once
more?" The relentlessly unflattering descriptions of life
at each of its stages, from childhood to "the wintry blast"
of old age, carry a heavy burden of regret and sadness.
But they also have, in their very extravagance, sparks of
vitality and wit that differentiate them from simple melancholy. Yeats's considerable acquaintance with mali-
cious public controversy brings special force to

> That defiling and disfigured shape
> The mirror of malicious eyes
> Casts upon his eyes until at last
> He thinks that shape must be his shape.

The diction in these first two stanzas of section 2 becomes
increasingly full of echoes. Two adjacent lines begin,
"What matter if"; "the unfinished man" of one line is
followed by "the finished man"; and the couplet rhyme
of "escape—shape" is used twice in six lines. The next-
to-last stanza opens with the reply to his own rhetorical
question, "What matter if I live it all once more?" He
answers: "I am content to live it all again / And yet again."
He accepts life despite his increasingly extravagant descriptions of life's wretchedness. Living men are like the
blind leading the blind and "shall fall into the ditch"
(Matthew 15:14 and Luke 6:39), but those foul ditches
are full of frog's eggs that symbolize fertility and vitality.
Then the poem shifts, with more dignified diction, to
the suffering of having wooed "a proud woman not kindred
to his soul"—here using "soul" in a generalized, conventional manner and not as *"My Soul."* This suffering
carries considerable poignancy in its echo of Yeats's tor-
tured love for Maud Gonne.

The opening statement of the last stanza, that "I am
content" to accept life, has the straightforward rhetorical
force of its repetition of the previous stanza's opening
and also considerable emotional impact as a reminder of

the sadness that he has found in life. Then follows a rich echoing of *My Soul*'s last stanza. *My Soul* had claimed that "the dead can be forgiven," but *My Self* will "forgive myself the lot!" *My Soul*'s flood of spiritual ecstasy will leave a man physically "stricken deaf and dumb and blind," but *My Self* gains, by casting out remorse, a sweetness that leads to laughter and song rather than to deafness and dumbness. Instead of *My Soul*'s blindness, *My Self* will achieve a state in which "everything we look upon is blest." The victory of *My Self*'s argument is clear, but the reader should notice—and admire—that the victory is achieved by rhetorical means and in spite of the un-attractive descriptions of life. *My Self* is willing to accept a life in which youth is ignominious and in which his wooing of a proud woman leads to suffering rather than to pleasure. His affirmation gains further force when in the final description of the sweetness achieved by the casting out of remorse, the pronoun changes from "I" to "we" and thus includes the reader.

The last word in this poem belongs literally and figuratively to *My Self* and not to *My Soul*. The triumph of that last word, "blest," is immediately confirmed in the opening lines of the poem that follows "A Dialogue of Self and Soul" in all printings, "Blood and the Moon": "Blessed be this place / More blessed. . . . "

"Coole and Ballylee, 1931"
(w. 1931–32, publ. 1932, *Poems* 243,
   CP 239[2])
and
"The Choice"
(w. 1931, publ. 1932, *Poems* 246, *CP* 242)

"Coole and Ballylee, 1931" is a poem of tribute to Lady Gregory and Coole Park. It developed from the similarly titled "Coole Park, 1929," which was published in 1931 as a preface to a short book of reminiscences by Lady

Gregory about Coole Park. Yeats said in February 1932, while he was at Coole and writing "Coole and Ballylee, 1931," that he was turning that earlier, relatively straightforward tribute "into a poem of some length—various sections with more or less symbolic matter."[3] He considered the possibility of combining the two poems,[4] and although the poems were kept separate, he always printed them next to each other. "Coole and Ballylee, 1931," however, takes a much more ambitious range of topics than the earlier poem.

The opening three stanzas of "Coole and Ballylee, 1931" make statements about the soul, not limited here to the dramatic opponent of *"My Self"* in "A Dialogue of Self and Soul," but instead with a broader, more traditional meaning. Those statements are made through emblems associated with Coole Park and Thoor Ballylee. The poem uses a stream at Thoor Ballylee to suggest the eternal soul's illusory disappearance at death, to be followed by the soul's eventual reappearance. This stream ends at a swallow hole or fissure in the limestone, half a mile beyond Thoor Ballylee in the general direction of Coole Park. Halfway to Coole Park, three miles to the southwest, a spring rises at a "rocky place"; those waters dip underground again for a quarter mile and then form the small Coole River, which feeds Coole Lake. The waters of the lake, in turn, "drop" back into the porous limestone. The poem assumes that this stream links Thoor Ballylee with Coole and thus metaphorically links Yeats with Lady Gregory.[5]

In the next two stanzas, a swan's sudden flight—like the mysterious dropping and reappearing waters—again reminds the poet of the disappearance and mysterious reappearance of the soul. These hints of the soul's immortality would have been comforting to Yeats, aged sixty-six, and to Lady Gregory, aged seventy-nine, who was suffering her painful last illness: "Sound of a stick upon the floor, a sound / From somebody that toils from chair to chair." Throughout the winter and spring of 1931–32, when this poem was being written, Yeats waited with her at Coole Park for her death, which came in May.

The swan also helps to reinforce the water's symbolic contrast with the barren "dry sticks under a wintry sun" that help to evoke a tragic mood. The "sudden thunder" of the swan's flight draws the poet's attention to the "glittering" expanse of "the flooded lake." The energy and loveliness of the swan, "that stormy white," sparks the poet's imagination and so restores him from "what knowledge or its lack had set awry." This restoration, even if only fleeting and even if limited to the poet, links directly with the subsequent allusions to cultivated, old-fashioned, romantic values that the poem associates with Coole Park. The arrogance of the swan's purity is here a highly favorable attribute and one that Lady Gregory and Yeats would each find consistent with their embattled circumstances.

The second half of this work praises the aristocratic traditions embodied by Lady Gregory and Coole Park, but a consistently melancholy note tolls in each of these stanzas. Lady Gregory is a "last inheritor," and the poem uses the past tense when referring to traditional, romantic values: Coole Park and houses like it "seemed once more dear than life." But now "all that great glory" is exhausted. Since April 1927, when Coole Park was purchased by the Irish Land Commission and Department of Forestry, Lady Gregory had been only a tenant in her own house. A governmental agency was not likely to appreciate the "beloved books" in the library Lady Gregory so highly prized, the "old marble heads," and "old pictures everywhere." And, in fact, at the estate auction at Coole Park three months after Lady Gregory died, and only six months before this poem was written, the 1,976 books auctioned from the eleven-foot-tall mahogany book cases of the library fetched an average of less than ten pence (twenty-one cents) each, and mirrors brought higher prices than oil paintings.[6] Coole Park's strong sense of place, so "rich in memory," contrasts forlornly with the nomadic present era, which is expressed in a simile that uses a desert setting—"like some poor Arab tribesman and his tent"—and continues an emphasis on the opposition between water and aridity.

Here, as a next-to-last stanza, came the eight lines that, after the first printing of the poem, Yeats removed and printed separately as "The Choice." These lines take as their subject the poet's decision to reject saintly "perfection of the life," which would lead to "a heavenly mansion," and instead to choose perfection of "the work"— and the eventual hollowness of that worldly achievement:

> The intellect of man is forced to choose
> Perfection of the life, or of the work,
> And if it take the second must refuse
> A heavenly mansion, raging in the dark.

Presumably, although the poem does not say so, worldly achievements could have been more satisfying if the old values represented by Coole Park had not faded. As "The Choice" now stands, however, its only links to "Coole and Ballylee, 1931" are the poet's joyless mood of wintry desolation (without the inspiration provided by the swan) and the poet's sorrow over the impending loss of this earthly mansion.

The famous last stanza of "Coole and Ballylee, 1931" turns more specifically to a poet's viewpoint and describes as "the last romantics"—Yeats, Lady Gregory, and probably the others who benefited from the steadying influence of Coole Park:

> We were the last romantics—chose for theme
> Traditional sanctity and loveliness;
> Whatever's written in what poets name

> The book of the people; whatever most can bless
> The mind of man or elevate a rhyme;
> But all is changed, that high horse riderless,
> Though mounted in that saddle Homer rode
> Where the swan drifts upon a darkening flood.

Their loyalty to the themes described here—"traditional sanctity and loveliness," the enduring wisdom of folklore, and a concern for elevating the mind of man—has made them aliens in the contemporary world where "all is changed," where a tradition has disappeared that had reached back to Homer and to Pegasus as a symbol of poetic genius. And with this melancholy evocation of the threatening world of the *Tower* poems, the reader moves to the ominous final line which recollects the swan and water images of the opening three stanzas: "Where the swan drifts upon a darkening flood."

"Byzantium"
(w. 1930, publ. 1932, *Poems* 248, *CP* 243)

A useful starting point for discussing this famous poem is the scholar and poet Jon Stallworthy's concluding remark to his careful study of the thirteen-page manuscript of the poem: "No matter from what angle one approaches Yeats's Byzantium, and many critics have travelled by many different routes, its magic and mystery defy definition, and at every point one is aware of other levels and areas of meaning, still unexplored, just beyond the range of sight."[7] I applaud Stallworthy's forthright acknowledgment of the complexity of "Byzantium," but after that I become restive about some of the particular sources of the keen admiration paid to this poem in virtually every published literary opinion. "Byzantium" is an intensely ambitious poem laced with magnificent phrases and lines, but there are some distinct limitations to its success.

Two factors that contribute indirectly to the reputation of the poem are the link with "Sailing to Byzantium" and the significance that Yeats's theory of history in *A Vision* (1925) affords Byzantium during the sixth and ninth centuries. Any reader who comes to "Byzantium" after having read "Sailing to Byzantium" will expect the poems to be related, and Yeats surely intended just that. His friend T. Sturge Moore had complained, in a letter of April 16, 1930, that the golden bird of "Sailing to Byzantium" was disappointingly close to the Nature from which the speaker of that poem sought escape. Yeats wrote the prose draft of "Byzantium" within two weeks of receiving that letter, and he later described the poem as further "exposition" of that golden bird. The third stanza of "Byzantium" substantiates that claim with the "miracle, bird or golden handiwork" which is "planted on the starlit golden bough" and which can crow like the cocks of Hades—presumably signaling the rebirth of day or of a life—or can "in glory of changeless metal" scorn "common bird or petal / And all complexities of mire or blood."

Yeats had mentioned a fascination with sixth-century Byzantium in *A Vision* (1925), a year before "Sailing to Byzantium" was written. He cited, as an example of perfected Byzantine art, the great domed cathedral of St. Sophia built by the Emperor Justinian in 537; Yeats specifically described it as a place appropriate to spiritual ecstasy.[8] Furthermore, Yeats associated that particular era in Byzantium's history with the fifteenth phase of the moon, in which beauty reaches absolute perfection and thus is outside human existence. All of this is particularly appropriate to "Sailing to Byzantium," in which the old man seeks to escape the ravages of time by becoming a part of perfect, timeless beauty. The sixth-century, "early" Byzantium that Yeats admired for its "unity of culture" is at least a close analogy to the imaginary setting for "Sailing to Byzantium."[9] Despite Yeats's habitual indifference to precise chronology, some caution is necessary about equating that sixth-century, early Byzantium with the city described in "Byzantium," whose prose draft reads: "Describe Byzantium as it is in the system towards the end of the first Christian millenium."[10] Byzantine art went into eclipse during the iconoclasm of the eighth century, but reasserted itself in the middle of the ninth century and was marked by splendor and orientalism. In *A Vision* Yeats discussed Byzantine civilization during the last portion of the first Christian millenium, focusing on the increasing predominance of the spiritual life over intellectual and physical life. The spiritual life in Byzantium, according to Yeats, had "little effect upon men's conduct" and was "perhaps a dream which passes beyond the reach of conscious mind but for some rare miracle or vision . . . like that profound reverie of the somnambulist which may be accompanied by a sensuous dream . . . and yet neither affect the dream nor be affected by it."[11] That "profound reverie of the somnambulist" accords well with much of "Byzantium," but does little to aid specific understanding of the poem, except insofar as the reader becomes more willing to expect vagueness. The prose draft has a list of objects encountered in the poem: "A walking mummy; flames at the street corners where the soul is purified. Birds of hammered gold singing in the golden trees. In the harbour [dolphins] offering their backs to the wailing dead that they may carry them to paradise."[12] And those intentions are reinforced by Yeats's discussion of the poem in his drafts of a lecture in 1932, when he described Byzantium as the "city where the saints showed their wasted forms upon a background of gold mozaic [sic]." He added, "In one poem I have pictured the ghosts swimming, mounted upon dolphins, through the sensual seas, that they may dance upon its pavements."[13]

"Byzantium" is without question a rich mine of the magnificent inventions of phrase that are perhaps Yeats's greatest poetic strength. Nearly every line of the poem, if read by itself, draws well-deserved admiration for its phrasing. And the poem offers a tantalizing promise of structure to integrate those lines. First, there is a strong suggestion of narrative through the five stanzas. The poem moves chronologically from the evening twilight, as "the unpurged images of day recede," to "midnight," when the ghostly guide appears. There is also a hint of pattern in the geographical movement through the city to the magical pavement where, at the edge of the sea, the dolphins deliver the spirits of the dead for purgation of the "bitter furies of complexity." The poem further suggests a careful attention to its structure by the emphatic repetition of "complexities" and "fury" (or "embittered") in stanzas 1, 3, 4, and 5. The fifth stanza then collects, in its first four lines, phrases from the previous stanzas. This final stanza's first line, "Astraddle on the dolphin's mire and blood," echoes the first stanza's "mire of human veins" and the third stanza's "mire or blood." The next two lines of the last stanza, "Spirit after spirit! The smithies break the flood, / The golden smithies of the Emperor," recall the third stanza's "golden handiwork" and "golden bough," as well as the fourth stanza's "spirits." The fourth line, "Marbles of the dancing floor," refers to "the Emperor's pavement" and echoes "dance," both in the fourth stanza. The poem's last line, "That dolphin-torn, that gong-tormented sea," includes the dolphins and the "flood" from the first lines of this stanza and the gong from the first stanza.

But despite these interweaving echoes of word and phrase, all five stanzas remain distinctly separate from one another and the connections between stanzas are obscure. The riddling syntax of the final stanza brings the poem to a conclusion that is full of verbal resonance, but that might also suggest the poet's control of images and words has been overwhelmed:

> Astraddle on the dolphin's mire and blood,
> Spirit after spirit! The smithies break the flood,
> The golden smithies of the Emperor!

> Marbles of the dancing floor
> Break bitter furies of complexity,
> Those images that yet
> Fresh images beget,
> That dolphin-torn, that gong-tormented sea.

It is reasonably certain that the "flood" refers collectively to the representatives of ordinary life: the unpurged spirits, the dolphins, and the sea, but with primary emphasis on these unpurged spirits as they arrive at Byzantium after riding on dolphins in the sea. This flood is brought under control by the emperor's smithies, who are corollary to the marbles of the dancing floor; the artisans and created patterns "break" the complexity of the unpurged world.

Before reaching the end of the sentence and of the poem the reader must confront two phrases that seem to be appositives and contain some echoes from earlier lines, but that cannot be assigned confidently to antecedents. The first of these appositives—"images that yet / Fresh images beget"—could refer to the "marbles of the dancing floor," which are instrumental in breaking the complexity of the arriving spirits into new, purged patterns or images. On the other hand, the "images that yet / Fresh images beget" could also refer to the mortal, procreative, unpurged world of complexity, which is antithetical to the artifice of Byzantium. The second appositive—"that dolphin-torn, that gong-tormented sea"— receives powerful rhetorical emphasis by being the final line of the poem and by its insistently repetitive structure that twice uses the demonstrative pronoun "that." The dolphins and the sea refer back to the "flood" and therefore to the unpurged spirits. The gong, as a reminder of time, also links with the mortal, unpurged existence that is subject to the tyranny of time. If the "images that yet / Fresh images beget" refer to the marbles of the dancing floor and if "that dolphin-torn, that gong-tormented sea" refers to the unpurged world, then the favorable con-

notation of "fresh images" and the unfavorable connotations of "torn" and "tormented" suggest that the purging
available in Byzantium is highly desirable. But if the
"images that yet / Fresh images create" and the sea both
refer to an unpurged life that is antithetical to Byzantium's ideal, then the conclusion of this poem gives so
much emphasis to mortal life as to undercut the value
of purgation from life's complexity.

Another problem—or opportunity—facing the reader
is the relative emphasis given to artistic creation as a
topic in the poem. I favor a more direct approach that
assumes the topic is the purgation that follows death.[14]
But some readers will prefer a more expansive view that
allows the underlying topic to be the creation of artistic
images from life. That approach has the advantage of
allowing the reader to find somewhat greater unity between the various stanzas, and, incidentally, between
the two Byzantium poems.[15] In that aesthetic view an
artist or poet can align himself, at least by analogy, with
the smithies and the marbles—with the divine or miraculous instruments of transformation—rather than
merely with the objects on which those transformations
are performed. And since this view depends upon analogy, it can be combined with the other approach without
necessarily losing any of its interest, as has been dem-
onstrated by several excellent critics, notably Richard
Ellmann and Helen Vendler.[16]

Words for Music Perhaps: I. "Crazy Jane
and the Bishop"
(w. 1929, publ. 1930, *Poems* 255, *CP* 251)

Yeats had been seriously ill in the winter of 1927–28 with
congestion of the lungs, influenza, and exhaustion and
then again in the winter of 1929–30 with Maltese fever.
In the 1933 dedication to *The Winding Stair and Other
Poems*, he recounted that after the second of those ill-

nesses he wrote "Byzantium" to warm himself "back into life" with a serious theme "that might befit my years."[17] But in the same dedication he also said that in the spring of 1929, after his recovery from the first of those illnesses, he had felt a much less dignified outburst of exuberance: "Life returned to me as an impression of the uncontrollable energy and daring of the great creators."[18] The poems that he wrote in that mood "sometimes came out of the greatest mental excitement I am capable of" and were fueled by sexual desire, as he later confided to Olivia Shakespear.[19]

The most famous of those poems are assigned to a wonderfully energetic old woman named Crazy Jane, a character who was, as Yeats said in a letter, "more or less founded" on an old peasant woman from a cottage outside Gort, the town near Coole Park. That woman, Yeats reported, "has an amazing power of acidulous speech—one of her queer performances is a description of how the meanness of a Gort shopkeeper's wife over the price of a glass of porter made her so despairing of the human race she got drunk. The incidents of that drunkenness are of an epic magnificence. She is the local satirist and a really terrible one."[20] Yeats had also acknowledged that same woman, known as "Cracked Mary," as the source of a song in his peasant drama, *A Pot of Broth*, first performed in 1902. In the song an old woman boldly announces her sexual desire for "poor Jack the journeyman."[21] The first published versions of "Crazy Jane and the Bishop," "Crazy Jane Grown Old Looks at the Dancers," and "Crazy Jane Reproved," used the name "Cracked Mary," but Yeats soon changed her name to "Crazy Jane," probably to avoid adding an echo of the Virgin Mary's name to the already vigorous anticlericism of these poems.[22] "Crazy Jane and the Bishop," dated March 2, 1929, is the first of the group and can serve as an example of the Crazy Jane poems. Two others were written later that month, followed by one in October,

and three more in 1931. After those seven poems, Yeats
had had enough. In the winter of 1931–32 he told his
wife, "I want to exorcise that slut, Crazy Jane, whose
language has become unendurable."[23]

Crazy Jane has delighted and fascinated nearly all
of Yeats's readers because of her lively extravagances of
desire and of language. This sprightly old woman expresses her unblushingly bold allegiance to sexuality
through affection for her lover, Jack the Journeyman,
and through absolute loyalty to him, even though he
never married her and even though he has died. As she
says in this first of her poems, "Jack had my virginity,"
and because "we lived like beast and beast," without
marriage, the local cleric banished her lover. Her allegiance to Jack and to physical passion also are expressed
in her unstinting antagonism for that cleric, who has since
become a bishop. She attacks his spiritual authority and
conventional social authority by viewing the bishop and
his religious paraphernalia merely from a physical point
of view. The bishop held an "old book"—the Bible—"in
his fist"; he has "a skin, God knows, / Wrinkled like the
foot of a goose"; and he has a "hunch upon his back."
By comparison, her "dear Jack that's dead" stood as straight
and tall as "a birch-tree."

The refrain, "The solid man and the coxcomb," clev-
erly plays upon the two meanings of "solid": sober and
serious (a "solid" citizen) or physically sturdy and strong.
In the first stanza Jane says that the bishop had called
Jack a "coxcomb," a fool, usually one who is foolishly
vain about his achievements. Thus, in the refrain the
"solid man" is the bishop and the "coxcomb" is Jack. But
those attributions are eventually reversed.[24] In the third
stanza, where the bishop's wrinkled skin and hunched
back are contrasted with Jack's "birch-tree" solidness
(and phallic erectness), Jack is now "the solid man" and
the bishop is "the coxcomb." That reversal is then further
complicated in the final stanza, which refers both to Jack's

past solidness ("Jack had my virginity") and to his present
lack of solidness, as a ghost wandering in the night and
seeking shelter under a blasted oak. Thus in the final
refrain Jack is both eligible and ineligible to be "the solid
man." The reader knows that to read the refrain as in
the first stanza—with the bishop as "the solid man" and
Jack as "the coxcomb"—remains distantly possible, though
now the refrain carries so much irony that the reader
can be certain that Crazy Jane wants to reverse the original refrain when she spits out this final line.

Her preference for Jack and her attack on the bishop
are stated with wonderful extravagance and are supported by nearly every detail of the poem. She speaks
every line, even though she and her adversary share the
title—"Crazy Jane and the Bishop." Crazy Jane's voice
can be heard in the earthy, lively diction, from "foot of
a goose" and "heron's hunch" to "I spit." The stoutly
pagan anticlericalism of her curses on the bishop is reinforced by the midnight setting, the wandering ghost of
her dead lover, and perhaps even the oak tree, which
was sacred to the pagan Druids. The section title for the
Crazy Jane poems, "Words for Music Perhaps," is appropriate to the ballad-like vigor of these short four-beat
lines, with their conspicuous adjacent rhymes (*aabccb*).
Nothing in the poem works in the bishop's favor. Crazy
Jane's hearty mastery of the situation can give the reader
the pleasing but unrealistic impression that Crazy Jane
would be indefatigable, no matter how complicated a
philosophical problem she might face.

Crazy Jane's vivacity is so appealing that some readers expect her to be an independent character who somehow possesses more insight and systematic wisdom than
can be found in her poems. Instead, the reader must be
content with the poems, and even then should notice
that some of her poems are so ambiguous that it would
be difficult to construct a "biography" of her from the
information given. For example, in "Crazy Jane Re-

proved," which immediately follows "Crazy Jane and the Bishop," the reader cannot be certain who speaks the verse. The dramatic situation in "Crazy Jane Reproved" could suggest that the verses, in which Crazy Jane is reproved, are spoken by someone like the bishop and that the nonsense refrain is Crazy Jane's scoffing reply. But the diction of the verses is far closer to Crazy Jane than to the bishop in expressions such as "thunder-stones," "that Heaven yawns," and "made the joints of Heaven crack."

Despite whatever limitations Crazy Jane might have, she drew considerable affection from Yeats. In 1934, two years after he had spoken of trying to "exorcise that slut, Crazy Jane" and had stopped writing Crazy Jane poems, Yeats wrote "A Prayer for Old Age." There he scorns intellectualism ("those thoughts men think / In the mind alone") and praises an earthiness that is reminiscent of Crazy Jane: "He that sings a lasting song / Thinks in a marrow-bone." That short poem ends with a prayer stating one of the important moods of his last years. He asks that his thoughts and his manner will not be those of "a wise old man," but instead "that I may seem, though I die old, / A foolish, passionate man." That lively, errant note persisted with "The Wild Old Wicked Man" in 1937 and "John Kinsella's Lament for Mrs. Mary Moore" in July 1938, the same month in which he paid Crazy Jane the poetical compliment of reviving her (and at least a memory of the bishop) for "Crazy Jane on the Mountain."

8

~~~~~~

An Old Man's
Eagle Mind: 1936–1939

By 1936, when Yeats fell very seriously ill, he had written enough fine poetry to place himself among the greatest poets of all time. But Yeats did not die in 1936. He recovered his health and went on for nearly three years that were marked by moments of energy so intense as to be distressing to the more polite of his readers. He was alienated from the liberal and socialist views that then held the fashion among many younger writers. The values he prized were not those of a coming era of egalitarianism and economic justice, but rather of an aristocratic past that now seemed to be echoed only by fascist dictators. Yeats refused to compromise his increasingly lonely standards and he was more than willing to shock his readers with the extremity of his opinions. To some extent he gave up hope of restoring the contemporary world to his values, but he did not choose to be silent. Alongisde those public issues was the private, inescapable fact that he was nearing death. Bodily decay had been a central subject in his poems of the 1920s, but now he faced a prospect of extinction rather than a mere weakening of his powers. All of this produced in his poetry a variety of responses that ranges from the transcendent orientalizing of "Lapis Lazuli" to the lusty Irish vigor of "John Kinsella's Lament for Mrs. Mary Moore" and from the imperious confidence of "Under Ben Bulben" to the unnerving uncertainty of "Man and the Echo."

Young writers such as W. H. Auden and Stephen Spender were deeply offended by Yeats's strident lack of sympathy for their efforts to make the modern world more just. Other readers were shocked by the old poet's frequent lapses into vulgarity on the subjects of sex and religion—and sometimes on both subjects at once. The extremes that energized Yeats's last years resulted in poetry that amply repays whatever questionable moments of social embarrassment or even moral disgust some readers might encounter.

New Poems (1938)

"Lapis Lazuli"
(w. 1936, publ. 1938, *Poems* 294, *CP* 291)

"Lapis Lazuli" is my choice as Yeats's finest poem. Its artistic success stems both from an ambitiously wide-ranging treatment of a serious topic—the necessity of accommodating oneself to tragic circumstances—and from a masterful employment of poetical rhetoric. The magnificently satisfying language at the end of the poem is enriched by its thoroughgoing contrast with the off-handed, brazenly informal diction in the opening stanza, which calls William of Orange "King Billy," and which adopts deliberately trite expressions such as "For everybody knows or else should know":

> I have heard that hysterical woman say
> They are sick of the palette and fiddle-bow,
> Of poets that are always gay,
> For everybody knows or else should know
> That if nothing drastic is done
> Aeroplane and Zeppelin will come out,
> Pitch like King Billy bomb-balls in
> Until the town lie beaten flat.

The extravagant casualness in this first stanza is all the more noticeable because the lack of high seriousness could easily be used as damning evidence against him by the women who charge that the gaiety of poets is inappropriate amidst the ominous threat of war. From these women's point of view, poets are useless, irresponsible, and perhaps even subversive.

"Lapis Lazuli" confidently answers those charges that art is frivolous and unsuited to desperate times. In a letter written three weeks after Yeats received this lapis lazuli carving, he announced that, in life, "the supreme aim is an act of faith and reason to make one rejoice in the midst of tragedy."[1] The defense of the arts in "Lapis Lazuli" depends upon showing the appropriateness of gaiety in tragic circumstances. Yeats's linking of gaiety with tragedy was an exaggeration, but it can be defended, for as the poem says, at the end of a Shakespearean tragedy the devastated hero faces death with a manner that, although not joyful, is at least not tearful; Hamlet and Lear at the moment of death "do not break up their lines to weep."

This paradoxical combination of joy and tragedy is best suited to nonlogical presentation, and that is the manner in which its powerful expression is achieved in "Lapis Lazuli." Yeats was fascinated with the "third eye" of Eastern mystics, which, as he had explained in the introduction to Shri Purohit Swami's *An Indian Monk* in 1932, is "no physical organ, but the mind's direct apprehension of the truth, above all antinomies."[2] The poem gives three instances of that nonlogical, but powerful, "direct apprehension of the truth": the gaiety of Shakespearean tragic characters, in the second stanza; the gaiety of those who build beautiful but impermanent things, in the third stanza; and, at the end of the poem, the gaiety of the Chinamen, who stare at a tragic scene.

"Tragic joy," as Yeats often referred to this paradoxical notion, was one of his most persistent ideas. As

early as 1904 he praised tragic drama's transcendence of
external circumstances—of "all that is created out of the
passing mode of society"—in reaching, at the moment
of a hero's death, "tragic joy and the perfectness of tragedy." He added that when we witness "tragic gaiety" in
the theater, "we rejoice in every energy, whether of
gesture, or of action, or of speech" that is associated with
it. In that moment, the "laws of Nature seem as unimportant in comparison as did the laws of Rome to" the
tragic hero "Coriolanus when his pride was upon him."[3]
Yeats thought that the effect of tragedy depended partly
upon its distance from the ordinary, daily world—about
which the "hysterical women" in the opening stanza of
"Lapis Lazuli" are so concerned—and that "the supreme
moment in tragic art" can be so startlingly powerful and
strange that it seems "unearthly."[4] This notion remained
one of his favorites. In 1937 he wrote, in "A General
Introduction for my Work," that "the heroes of Shakespeare convey to us . . . the sudden enlargement of their
vision, their ecstasy at the approach of death. . . . No
actress has ever sobbed when she played Cleopatra, even
the shallow brain of a producer has never thought of such
a thing."[5] And in 1938 he insisted: "The arts are all the
bridal chamber of joy. No tragedy is legitimate unless it
leads some great character to his final joy," as in "Hamlet's speech over the dead Ophelia" or "Lear's rage under
the lightning."[6]

Shakespearean tragedy, in which Yeats discovered
a combination of courage and ecstatic insight, thus provided an example of gaiety that is coexistent with, and
even essential to, the highest moments of tragedy. In
answering the charges leveled against art by the women
of the first stanza, examples culled from Shakespeare are
particularly useful since the women (and readers of the
poem) would be familiar with Shakespearean tragedy and
would respect it.

Richard Ellmann has pointed out that the association

of gaiety and Shakespearean tragedy in the second stanza is peculiarly "Western," as opposed to the peculiarly Oriental or "Eastern" fourth and fifth stanzas.[7] The intervening third stanza, which points to the inevitable destruction of each successive civilization, mediates between the "Western" and "Eastern" portions of the poem. Such a progression helps to bridge the startling leaps in subject matter from the contemporary scene in the first stanza to the Shakespearean tragic ecstasy in the second stanza, and then to the procession of civilizations and the example of the little-known Greek sculptor Callimachus in the third stanza, before the Chinese scene in the concluding two stanzas.

Yeats discussed the difference between Western and Eastern attitudes toward tragedy just two days after he had received the eighteenth-century Chinese lapis lazuli carving for which the poem is titled. This hard-stone carving, eleven inches high, shows a mountain scene much like that described in the poem. It was given to Yeats in 1935 as a splendid seventieth-birthday gift by a wealthy young English poet, Henry (Harry) Talbot de Vere Clifton, to whom the poem is dedicated. Yeats described the lapis lazuli carving to his poet friend Dorothy Wellesley and then made these fragmentary remarks:

Eternal theme of the sensual east. The heroic cry in the midst of despair. But no, I am wrong, the east has its solutions always and therefore knows nothing of tragedy. It is we, not the east, that must raise the heroic cry.[8]

Yeats often compared those Western and Eastern views in ways that are generally important to this poem, despite the difficulty of reducing his opinions to clear statements. He thought that the Western mind, which is characterized by intellectual pride and optimism, views the history of successive civilizations as a continuing progression toward mankind's eventual conquest of the forces of nature.

This Western emphasis on the progress of entire civilizations rather than on the plight of each individual mortal is paralleled, to some extent, by Christianity's focus on heaven as an escape from the problems of individual mortal existence. Theoretically, a Christian should even welcome death. Thus Yeats can say that the West, because of its ultimate disregard for mortal life, finds solutions in an afterlife (or in a moment of transcendent ecstasy), outside the sphere of human action. But the East has solutions that effortlessly incorporate the individual within a system that includes all of mortal nature and the ageless heavens. The East, according to Yeats, rejects intellectual pride and optimism as trivial and is indifferent to history. The West is assertive, proud, and organized; the East is content to be part of the natural world and is humble and spontaneous.[9]

After the Western topics of the first two stanzas, the poem begins to shift attention away from Europe. In the opening of the third stanza, the long parade of destroyed civilizations points out the transience of every civilization, including, of course, the contemporary European civilization about which the women in the first stanza are so concerned.

> On their own feet they came, or on shipboard,
> Camel-back, horse-back, ass-back, mule-back,
> Old civilisations put to the sword.
> Then they and their wisdom went to rack.

Yeats insisted, in his controversial introduction to the *Oxford Book of Modern Verse* in 1936, that because "all skill is joyful," a poet or artist should not be overwhelmed by the knowledge that his life and even his entire civilization would eventually end. Yeats believed that none of the arts should take "passive suffering" for a theme: "In all the great tragedies, tragedy is a joy to the man who dies; in Greece the tragic chorus danced."[10]

The remainder of the third stanza gives a specific example of the artist's proper gaiety in the face of the inevitable transience of man's accomplishments. Callimachus (often transliterated as "Callimachos" or "Kallimachos") was a Greek sculptor of the fifth century B.C., known for his skill with the running drill, a tool that allows a sculptor to carve more intricate drapery than is possible with a chisel. His graceful bronze lamp chimney in the shape of a palm tree, mentioned in the poem, stood in the Erechtheum on the Acropolis in Athens for at least six centuries, a time the poem compresses metaphorically to "but a day." Callimachus' mixture of Western and Eastern styles might explain Yeat's choice of so obscure a sculptor for this stanza where the poem moves from Western views to an Eastern perspective. As early as 1916, Yeats considered Callimachus' sculpture to be transitional between an earlier Ionic or "Eastern" style and a later Doric or "Western" style: "In half-Asiatic Greece Callimachus could still return to a stylistic management of the falling folds of drapery. . . . He was an archaistic workman . . . a momentary dip into ebbing Asia."[11]

Then, in a shift that is every bit as abrupt and startling as those between each of the three previous stanzas, the poem turns to the Chinese lapis lazuli carving. The brief fourth stanza describes the scene shown on the carving, and then the final stanza gives a meditative comment, which, just as in the stanzas on Shakespearean tragedy and on Callimachus, makes what would seem an unsubstantiated assertion that gaiety is an appropriate response to tragic circumstances.

After the statement of the women's charges against art in the opening stanza, the reader might reasonably expect that the remainder of the poem would defend art against those charges. These radical shifts of subject between stanzas compound the difficulty the reader faces in attempting to discover a pattern into which to fit the series of ambiguous, illogical statements found in the poem. The reader faces these challenges as early as the opening line of the second stanza, "All perform their tragic play." Here the reader must choose between the contradictory meanings of "play" as either "drama" or "frolic." The latter, "frolic," would seem to be immediately proved wrong, but then increasingly demands equal status, at first from the mocking diction of "struts" in the next line and then with the emphatic repetition of "gay / Gaiety": "Hamlet and Lear are gay; / Gaiety transfiguring all that dread." All of this is unexpected because the reader knows that *Hamlet* and *Lear* are tragedies, not comedies, just as, in the first stanza, the reader knew that the women's concern about the dire threat of war facing Europe in the mid-1930s was fully merited.

The reader's puzzlement is further compounded in the third stanza at lines 31–32 and 33–34, where, in two consecutive and parallel rhythmic units, a caesura jarringly halts the graceful sweep of a pair of run-on lines describing the marvelously beautiful handiwork of Callimachus. The first caesura comes before "stands" and the second before "stood but a day":

> Made draperies that seemed to rise
> When sea-wind swept the corner, stands;
> His long lamp chimney shaped like the stem
> Of a slender palm, stood but a day.

That powerful emphasis on the destruction of the artist's works is redoubled in the very next line ("All things fall") and logically leads the reader to expect artists to be sad because all their beautiful accomplishments will be destroyed. But the final word of the stanza overturns that expectation: "All things fall and are built again / And those that build them again are gay."

These confoundings of the reader's logical expectations each focus on the word "gay," and in each case

that key word has the emphasis of standing at the end
of a line and of being rhymed: "Of poets that are always
gay"; "They know that Hamlet and Lear are gay"; and
"And those that build them again are gay." Those patterns of form and sound, which are part of the poetical
rhetoric, are enhanced by the absence of any other easily
perceivable logic that could explain the choice of the
word "gay."

The final stanza similarly confuses the reader with
a combination of sadness and gaiety by announcing, in
the fifth line from the end, that the mountain scene is
"tragic" and appropriate for "mournful" music, mentioned in the next line:

> On all the tragic scene they stare.
> One asks for mournful melodies.

This sadness seems to contradict the tranquil description
in the previous fifteen lines, which include a clear and
logical explanation of how the carved mountain can effortlessly integrate, as a part of the carved landscape,
"every accidental crack or dent" that Western readers
would consider defects or damage. And then, in the
deservedly famous final lines, after the reader has accepted the mood as "tragic" and "mournful," comes what
logically ought to be yet another unexpected shock: the
confident announcement, in the last word of the poem,
that the Chinamen's ancient eyes, glittering—as the reader
would assume, because they are glazed with tears—are
not "sad," but gay:

> Their eyes mid many wrinkles, their eyes,
> Their ancient, glittering eyes, are gay.

These lines are miraculous not merely for their majestic,
reiterative pacing, but also because they succeed so perfectly in making the reader accept the expressive logic

of sounds, which, in turn, allows the reader to accept and even to savor the final word, "gay." Everyone, including those readers who are certain that this "gay" has no logical connection with the Western first three stanzas, is compelled by the poetical rhetoric to accept the irrational assertion that the Chinamen's eyes are gay.

The point, then, is whether this poem should be praised only for its magnificent ending, or whether the entire poem contributes to that success. Certainly, most of what "Lapis Lazuli" accomplishes is done with words, rhythms, and repetition rather than with logical presentation of ideas. The women of the first stanza might withdraw their objections if they themselves could be led to experience this compelling, albeit irrational gaiety. Oriental art expects the imaginative participation of its audience, and this poem about a Chinese art object leads the reader to experience "direct apprehension of the truth." That is what the poem achieves when the reader accepts its final word, "gay." Yeats had said, as early as 1916, that he preferred imaginative, even visionary arts that "enable us to pass for a few moments into a deep of the mind that had hitherto been too subtle for our habitation." He added, on that occasion (just before, incidentally, his first published mention of Callimachus), "It may be well if we go to school in Asia."[12]

"Tragic gaiety," the subject of "Lapis Lazuli," is a seemingly inexpressible and illogical mood, but the poem succeeds in expressing it. The rhetorical persuasiveness of the ending, on which syntax lays much emphasis and on which the rhythms invite the reader to rest, allows the reader to experience, if only for a lingering moment, an accommodation—like that of Shakespearean tragic characters, like that of Callimachus and of all artists, and like that of the Chinamen—to the terrible and tragic world they and all readers inhabit. History is on the side of the women in the opening stanza, but the power of this great rhetorical poem permits the reader to ignore the limited perspective of those women and to adopt the gaiety of all the others.

"An Acre of Grass"
(w. 1936, publ. 1938, *Poems* 301, *CP* 299)

Alongside the magnificent public poems like "Lapis Lazuli," Yeats wrote poems with an intensely personal focus, such as "An Acre of Grass" and "What Then?" The first poem places Yeats in the quiet, midnight setting of his suburban Dublin house. Nothing disturbs the serenity of his "old house / Where nothing stirs but a mouse."

The first half of the poem presents an ordinary, even stereotypical view of old age, according to which, the quieting of an old man's body, imagination, and mind is inevitable and therefore should be accepted calmly. The old man's serenely inactive mind is no longer beset by imagination, described unfavorably as "loose" or vagrant and irresponsible. He is no longer consuming the "rag and bone" materials from the junk heap of life. Old age may have cost him a decline of physical prowess, but has freed him of any temptation to commit his still unnamed, but apparently disreputable, former activity. Thus the reader is surprised to learn, at the end of this half of the poem, that the former activity of the old man's imagination and mind had been to "make the truth known." But the quiet tone and setting suggest that he has accepted, perhaps with no stronger feeling than regret, the limits that old age has imposed on him.

Then, at the opening of the poem's second half, the tone immediately shifts. The narrator speaks of "frenzy" rather than the passivity that the reader had been led to expect from the first half. In place of that earlier decorousness, the poem now admires the examples of Timon of Athens, King Lear, William Blake, and Michelangelo.

Shakespeare's Timon of Athens is an embittered misanthrope whose famous epitaph chimes interestingly against Yeats's equally famous epitaph at the end of "Under Ben Bulben":

> Cast a cold eye
> On life, on death,
> Horseman, pass by!

Timon's epitaph ends: "Pass by and curse thy fill, but pass and stay not here thy gait."[13] Yeats, who admired the energy and purity of such dramatic extremes of emotion, cited Timon's epitaph as one of the "eternal gestures" of life, whose "energy" is "eternal delight" rather than sorrow.[14] Similarly, *King Lear*, and especially the old king's rage and madness during the storm in Act III, was a lifelong favorite of Yeats because of its "imaginative wildness" and "delight in passions that seemed all but too great for human life."[15] William Blake, the third of these four violent old men, thought that "enthusiastic hatred" was much preferable to any "mildness founded upon unbelief and cowardice," as Yeats repeatedly emphasized in a biographical sketch written in 1893.[16] Michelangelo's stupendous fresco decorations of the Sistine Chapel include the sublime power of the ceiling (1508–12) and the tumultuous frenzy of the dead in the *Last Judgment* (1536–41), completed when he was sixty-six; Michelangelo lived to eighty-nine. The nudity displayed in his *Last Judgment* was so bold that, within thirty years, two popes had ordered artists to paint strategically located pieces of drapery on many of the figures in Michelangelo's painting.

The second half of the poem admires the truth associated with William Blake's energy—he "beat upon the wall / Till truth obeyed his call"—and the "frenzy" of Michelangelo's mind, as expressed in his painting of

The Last Judgment. The words "truth" and "frenzy," here associated with achievement, are repetitions from lines 12 and 13, where they were the first hints of the poet's startlingly energetic dismissal of the expected tranquility of old age. The conjunction of "truth" and "frenzy" is the main point of the poem and remained a goal of Yeats's final years. Without the frenzy that allows an old man to "make the truth known," he would justifiably be forgotten by mankind and condemned to the silence of his isolated retreat amidst its acre of grass. But if he adopts the violent, predatory energy of an eagle, he can succeed. The extraordinary distance in tone between the title, "An Acre of Grass," and the final line, "An old man's eagle mind," has thus been bridged, and the poet's choice of frenzy rather than serenity has been both explained and exemplified in the poem.

"What Then?"
(1937, *Poems* 302, *CP* 299)

Yeats's adamant refusal, in "An Acre of Grass," to accept a decorous, croquet-playing dotage was more than mere brazenness. It included a cry against the terrifying menace of a ghostly voice that he encounters in the next of these autobiographical poems, "What Then?"

The previous poem is based on the contrast between sedate quiet and energetic frenzy. Contrast is again essential to "What Then?"—where the title, a refrain spoken by Plato's ghost, devastatingly undercuts the smug and often trite assertions of each verse. There is, however, another contrast here. The deliberately banal diction in the earlier verses ("chosen comrades," "a famous man," "certain years," "sufficient money," and "friends that have been friends indeed") stands in sharp highlight against the noble dignity of the assertion in the final verse: "I swerved in nought, / Something to perfection brought." The smugness of those opening verses is accentuated by the wonderfully comic paralleling and therefore near equation of "plum and cabbage" with "Poets and Wits," in the third stanza.

The final verse surmounts the undercutting diction of "boyish" in "the work is done . . . / According to my boyish plan," and then rises to a note of confidence and dignity that usually would draw admiration: "Let the fools rage, I swerved in naught, / Something to perfection brought." But the reader already knows, both from the title and from the refrain, that the ghost is likely to have the last word. And, in fact, the ghost responds to the heightened confidence of the last verse by singing even more loudly his undercutting question, "What then?"— a question that has become increasingly more difficult for the reader to ignore as the verses progress from boyhood to maturity and then, in the final verse, to old age.

That the voice should be Plato's adds philosophical authority to the questioning. Yeats was more interested in the neo-Platonists than in Plato, who was suspicious of poetry and who banned from his ideal republic all poems except those that directly served individual and social morality. But the neo-Platonists and Plato together insisted on the supremacy of the ideal over even the most magnificent worldly achievements. Yeats mentioned in *A Vision* (1925) that when Plato separated "the Eternal Ideas from Nature," worldly life no longer could have absolute value. Thus the mention of Plato in the poem undercuts the poet's worldly accomplishments and increases the poignancy of the message. The same passage in *A Vision* demonstrates Yeats's awareness of the ideal and his simultaneous devotion to worldly existence: "To die into the truth" as Plato did "is still to die."[17]

"The Municipal Gallery Re-visited"
(1937, *Poems* 319, *CP* 316)

"The Municipal Gallery Re-visited" is another strongly personal poem. It mentions or alludes to some thirteen paintings in Dublin's Municipal Gallery of Modern Art, but the paintings have little importance in the poem beyond simply announcing their subjects and, to a lesser extent, their painters. What matters instead is the impact—on the poet—of those subjects and painters. The poem would hardly be changed if, instead of having paintings remind him of those subjects and painters, he had found them listed in an unillustrated catalog of the gallery or in a dictionary of recent Irish history. Only "Antonio Mancini's portrait of Augusta Gregory" has its painter explicitly named and only that painting has its artistic quality judged—and then not especially favorably. The poem carefully distances John Synge's extravagant and unmerited praise of that painting by using direct quotation: " 'Greatest since Rembrandt,' according to John Synge." And then Synge's opinion is immediately countered by a tactful corrective from the poet: "A great ebullient portrait certainly." In fact, Mancini's half-length oil portrait of Lady Gregory is Rembrandt-esque only in the heavy shadows that obscure much of the portrait, including the entire right half of Lady Gregory's sketchily delineated face. The painting further suffers from the heavy lines of a checkerboard grid that Mancini used as an aid in drawing.

Yeats's emotional response, which is the real subject of the poem, extended beyond the subjects shown in the paintings and included the painters. He knew Mancini and each of the five other artists whose paintings are mentioned in the poem; one was his father, J. B. Yeats, and another, Charles Shannon, was a friend for almost forty years who had died just five months before the poem was written. In a speech in 1937 he explained the origin of the poem:

For a long time I had not visited the Municipal Gallery. I went there a week ago and was restored to many friends. I sat down, after a few minutes, overwhelmed with emotion. There were pictures painted by men, now dead, who were once my intimate friends. There were portraits of my fellow-workers. . . . [18]

That deeply emotional reaction is directly conveyed in the poem:

> Around me the images of thirty years
> . . . .
> Heart-smitten with emotion I sink down,
> My heart recovering with covered eyes;
> Wherever I had looked I had looked upon
> My permanent or impermanent images.

The emphasis is very much on these images as images that belong to Yeats—"My . . . images"—and on the emotional reaction that these images evoke from him now. His personal presence dominates, and is far more important than anything else in the poem. In fact, so little information is given about one of the paintings that scholars can do little more than guess about the identity of either the sitter or the painter of the portrait:

> Before a woman's portrait suddenly I stand,
> Beautiful and gentle in her Venetian way.
> I met her all but fifty years ago
> For twenty minutes in some studio.

What matters is the poet's present reaction to the portrait; whether or not this refers to John Singer Sargent's oil portrait of Lady Charles Beresford is unimportant. The poem's tightly personal focus allows these images much less independent existence than is the case with the images recounted in "Beautiful Lofty Things," another poem written in 1937, in which the individuals praised by the poet receive at least as much emphasis as the poet's controlling judgment. In "The Municipal Gallery Re-visited" the paintings serve only to trigger his strongly felt sense of loss, which is the subject of the poem.

Last Poems (1939)

"Politics" and "Under Ben Bulben"
(both w. 1938, publ. 1939, *Poems* 348, 325;
  CP 337, 341)

Most readers who know "Under Ben Bulben" from the *Collected Poems* (1950, 1956) will expect to find "Under Ben Bulben" at the end rather than the beginning of Yeats's *Last Poems*. Yeats, however, specifically wanted to place "Under Ben Bulben" at the opening of *Last Poems* and to close the volume with a sprightly little lyric, "Politics" (w. 23 May 1938). His instructions were carried out in the Cuala Press limited edition *Last Poems and Two Plays* (July 1939) and in the most recent edition, *The Poems: A New Edition* in 1983.

Five months after Yeats's death, the editor who was preparing the Macmillan edition of *Last Poems & Plays* suggested to Mrs. Yeats that "Under Ben Bulben" be moved to the end of the volume. She accepted his recommendation,[19] and the revised order was used in all subsequent editions until 1983. Mrs. Yeats agreed to move the poem probably so that its serious tone could supplant the gaily irreverent note on which her husband wanted to end the volume. To her, "Politics" must have seemed too frivolous to stand as the last poem in her husband's final book. In "Politics," the poet asks: "How can I," with "that girl standing there, / My attention fix

/ On . . . politics?" And then, after admitting that "maybe
what they say is true / Of war and war's alarms," he ends
the poem with the human candor of

> But O that I were young again
> And held her in my arms.

But there is a discoverable logic to the order that
Yeats wanted. In his scheme, the final three poems are
"Man and the Echo," "The Circus Animals' Desertion,"
and "Politics." The first of those poems ends in terror
and the second poem ends in open-eyed, serious attentiveness to unadorned life—"the foul rag-and-bone shop
of the heart"—which provides the materials for art. In
that context the lusty hope of "Politics" becomes more
than merely a whimsical reminder of the poet's lingering
sexual desire; it is a poignant celebration of life.

Yeats's editor and Mrs. Yeats did not necessarily
show poor judgment, however, for "Under Ben Bulben"
was well suited as a final poem. Yeats himself selected
it as the program piece for the book that he may well
have guessed would be his last. In August 1938, within
half a year of his death, he began the poem by first writing
its famous, concluding epitaph, whose first version was
titled "Horse man" and ended with an echo of the *abi
viator* (go hence, traveler) motif from Jonathan Swift's
epitaph, which Yeats strongly admired. That first version
of Yeats's epitaph read:

> Draw rein; draw breath.
> Cast a cold eye
> On life, on death.
> Horse man pass by.[20]

Yeats made some corrections to "Under Ben Bulben" on
his deathbed in France,[21] and Mrs. Yeats took special
pains to have "Under Ben Bulben" published in three

Irish newspapers soon after his death, as a memorial poem and as an emphatic announcement of his wish to be buried in Ireland. After World War II, Yeats's body was returned to Ireland and reinterred at Drumcliff churchyard in full accordance with the instructions of the poem's final stanza:

> Under bare Ben Bulben's head
> In Drumcliff churchyard Yeats is laid.
> An ancestor was rector there
> Long years ago; a church stands near,
> By the road an ancient Cross.
> No marble, no conventional phrase,
> On limestone quarried near the spot
> By his command these words are cut:
> > Cast a cold eye
> > On life, on death.
> > Horseman, pass by!

The epitaph in the final three lines of "Under Ben Bulben" is, like the entire poem, an imperious command. The pronoun "I," used prominently in "Politics," is entirely absent from "Under Ben Bulben." The stern, dispassionate voice of the final section goes so far as to refer to Yeats in the third person: "In Drumcliff churchyard Yeats is laid" and "By his command these words are cut." But the injunction to "Cast a cold eye / On life, on death" need not entail a nihilistic dismissal of life or a brazen neglect of death. Rather, the epitaph tells the passerby to retain control of his demeanor in spite of a full recognition that neither aging nor death is subject to mortal command. The proud voice of "Under Ben Bulben" has no solutions, but speaks without a tremor of nervousness or fear. Its decorousness is reinforced by being addressed to a "horseman," which echoes the mythic Irish horsemen of section 1 and indirectly suggests the high esteem paid by ancient heroic societies and aristocratic modern societies to rigorous standards of conduct

and to horsemanship. Yeats exemplified decorousness,
even though his horsemanship fell far short of the standards expected of the heroic Irish Fianna or of the hard-
riding sons of the Anglo-Irish Ascendency—in his boyhood
he rode a small red pony, and in his old age he read
popular Westerns.

Some philosophical support for casting a cold eye
on death is available in the survival of the individual
soul, discussed in sections 1 and 2, though without in-
voking the particular authority of Hindu or Christian
doctrine. The poem simply says:

> Many times man lives and dies
> . . . .
> A brief parting from those dear
> Is the worse man has to fear.

The resolute tone of the poem suggests that even without
this philosophical comfort, the same strict standard of
conduct would be demanded.

The specifically Irish locale of the epitaph establishes that the immediate audience for "Under Ben Bulben" is an audience of Irishmen. Irish references, along
with more general ones, are discovered in section 1 (the
horsemen, probably the Fianna, and the superhuman
women, perhaps of the Tuatha de Danaan, who "ride
the wintry dawn / Where Ben Bulben sets the scene"),
in section 2 ("And ancient Ireland knew it all"), in section
3 (John Mitchel, the Irish revolutionary), in section 5
("Irish poets" and "the indomitable Irishry"), and in section 6 ("Under bare Ben Bulben's head / In Drumcliff
churchyard"). The specifically Irish audience of the epitaph, its imperious tone, and the goal it seeks are an-
ticipated in the final couplet of section 5: "That we in
coming days may be / Still the indomitable Irishry." This
is the pronouncement of a nobly indomitable Irish poet
near his death.

"Long-legged Fly"
(w. 1938, publ. 1939, *Poems* 339, *CP* 327)

The contrast in tone between "Politics" and "Under Ben Bulben" amply testifies to the wide range of Yeats's mind in his final years. His undiminished skill at his craft of verse may be readily seen in the fascinating structural resonance of "Long-legged Fly" and the vigorous ballad "John Kinsella's Lament for Mrs. Mary Moore," particularly if careful heed is paid to the refrains of those two poems.

"Long-legged Fly" poses an intriguing instance of Yeats's elaborate attentiveness to transitions and the expressive interrelationship between the parts of a poem. In 1936 he said that "the relation of all the elements to one another" in a poem should become apparent to the reader, at least "when the whole is finished." And he took his friend Ezra Pound to task for ignoring that precept in the *Cantos*, about which Yeats complained: "There is no transmission through time, we pass without comment from ancient Greece to modern England, from modern England to medieval China. . . . Like other readers I discover at present merely exquisite or grotesque fragments. . . . Even where there is no interruption he is often content, if certain verses and lines have style, to leave unbridged transitions, unexplained ejaculations, that make his meaning unintelligible."[22]

"Long-legged Fly" is among the most tightly designed of all Yeats's poems, yet the relationship between its parts is very much less clear than the careful structure of the poem would suggest. Each of the three stanzas has eight lines and a two-line refrain. Each stanza opens with the same word and with a two-line statement of consequences that depend upon careful maintenance of silence, as the reader is instructed to do in the third and fourth lines of each stanza:

> Quiet the dog, tether the pony
> To a distant post.
> . . . .
> Move most gently if move you must
> In this lonely place.
> . . . .
> Shut the door of the Pope's chapel,
> Keep those children out.

The remaining half of each stanza, exclusive of the refrain, describes a famous person, but in each case the person is seen in a pose that would be comically unsuitable for a public statue. The first stanza shows Caesar, an exemplar of military and civic power. But instead of riding at the head of his legions he is alone in his tent, musing or daydreaming, with "his eyes fixed upon nothing, / A hand under his head." In the second stanza an allusion to Troy's "topless towers" (from Marlowe's *Dr. Faustus*) identifies Helen of Troy, a paragon of female beauty and the inspiration for the Trojan legends, which Yeats considered the foundation of Greek culture. The poem catches Helen in the extreme awkwardness of early adolescence ("part woman, three parts child") practicing "a tinker shuffle / Picked up on the street." Tinkers are of a low and disreputable social class; Helen is practicing a "shuffle" rather than a dance; and, to emphasize those lowly origins, she has picked it up "on the street." In the third stanza, Michelangelo is painting the world-famous Sistine Chapel ceiling frescoes, which depict powerful figures in colossal proportions. But his own actions contrast sharply with the vigor of the frescoes. Atop the scaffolding he reclines on his back, as though resting, and paints with brush strokes that move as quietly as mice.

The parallelism between stanzas extends even to the careful limitation of Caesar's actions to "his eyes" and "hand," of Helen's action to "her feet," and of Michelangelo's action to "his hand." To all of this elaborate detail must be added the single most obvious signal of parallelism, the refrain that ends each stanza.

Yeats's already-quoted remarks about the *Cantos* suggest that he would expect the reader to notice these many parallels in "Long-legged Fly" and to interpret them as unmistakable evidence of "the relations of all the elements to one another." Thus the reader should expect that the detailed parallels between stanzas have a discoverable logic. At the very least, it should be possible to determine whether the refrain has a thematic connection with each stanza or is merely a deliberately nonsensical rhythmic interlude, like "Barrum, barrum, barrum," the refrain of a song in his play *The Resurrection* (1931),[23] or like "O my dear, O my dear," the refrain of "The Three Bushes" (1936).

Because the gender of the pronoun in the refrain changes to correspond to the character in that stanza, there must be a meaningful connection between the refrain and rest of the poem. The title of the poem further suggests the importance of the refrain, for the long-legged fly is encountered only in the title and the refrain. This small, aquatic insect (known variously as a "water strider," "pond skater," or "water-measurer") is found, from late spring until early fall, on the surface of streams, ponds, ditches, and lakes throughout Ireland and Great Britain. Some 350 species of the family Gerriade are distributed across the temperate and tropical regions of the world. The light, agile water strider uses its long, slender legs to stand atop the water's surface and then to dart silently and swiftly across the surface of the water, supported by surface tension.

At one time I delighted in the impish notion that the real subject of the poem might be just what its title says, the long-legged fly. Perhaps Caesar, Helen, and Michelangelo have been enlisted merely to help describe the long-legged fly, whose silent darting must have fascinated Yeats as it has so many other observers (including scientists who have made detailed studies of how this insect propels itself). Could it be that the poem deliberately transfers the awe that the reader would normally have for Caesar, Helen, and Michelangelo to a description of how this little insect moves? But that amusing speculation is unfounded, as remarks by Yeats's friend Edith Shackleton Heald testify. She recalled that Yeats was willing at least to consider supplanting the long-legged fly with "a kind of water-tortoise" he saw at the edge of a garden pool in Sussex. According to her account in a radio interview, Yeats asked Dorothy Wellesley if this tortoise could swim:

She said "Oh yes, I suppose so." He said "Could I see it?" and she said "Yes—let's throw it in." And she asked me to throw it in and I did and it began to swim, but rather laboriously, it seemed, towards the shore. And Yeats said "No—I don't think it'll do." Afterwards, when we had come back home, he read the rough draft of a poem—this poem he'd been thinking about, called "The Long-legged Fly".

In the same interview Edith Shackleton Heald went on to give the conventional interpretation that the subject of the poem is "the necessity of silence and peace to people of creative energy" and that the movement of a long-legged fly across the water resembles "the way the creative mind moves upon silence."[24]

With some reluctance I admit that she is probably correct. Even so, a careful consideration of the refrain can allow some room for fancy. The first line of each refrain, "Like a long-legged fly upon the stream," assigns the long-legged fly as one term in a simile whose other part, found in the second line of the refrain, is the "mind" of Caesar or Helen or Michelangelo. The extent to which those two parts of a simile are developed does not necessarily determine their relative importance, for in an epic simile, where the difference in length is extremely large, the longer one merely serves to illuminate the shorter. Thus perhaps the larger number of lines given in the poem to Caesar or Helen or Michelangelo need not necessarily diminish the worth of the long-legged fly. At any rate, the refrain in "Long-legged Fly" is certainly more substantial than "Barrum, barrum, barrum" or "O my dear, O my dear." It is an important image—perhaps even the most important one in the poem—and can serve as a nucleus for discovering additional levels of meaning.

"John Kinsella's Lament for Mrs. Mary Moore"
(1938, *Poems* 342, *CP* 329 [another version])

Yeats's use of the refrain in "Long-legged Fly" is related to his renewed interest in the ballad form during the 1930s. With help from Fred Higgins and Dorothy Wellesley, he edited two series of ballad broadsides, published by the Cuala Press as monthly sheets and then collected in annual volumes for 1935 and 1937. Each sheet had lively, hand-colored illustrations, and, to emphasize that ballads are meant to be sung, each ballad was accompanied by either a musical score or the name of its traditional tune.

One descendant of that broadside ballad lineage is "John Kinsella's Lament for Mrs. Mary Moore," which began in Yeats's mind with a refrain, as Yeats reported in a letter: "I have just thought of a chorus for a ballad. A strong [that is, prosperous] farmer is mourning over the shortness of life and changing times, and every stanza ends 'What shall I do for pretty girls now my old bawd is dead?' "[25]

In "John Kinsella's Lament for Mrs. Mary Moore" the power of the refrain shows itself by overturning the apparent meaning of the final stanza. In the two preceding stanzas, John Kinsella's rousing praise of Mary Moore's talents as a lover, cook, and drinking companion correspond perfectly with the refrain: "What shall I do

for pretty girls / Now my old bawd is dead?" Then the
poem shifts to a religious consolation that is reasonably
orthodox—even if John Kinsella states the Christian doctrine in somewhat comic language:

> I have heard it said in chapel
>   That but for Adam's sin
> Eden's Garden should still be there
>   And I be there within.
> No expectations fail there
>   No pleasing habits end,
> No man grows old, no girl grows cold,
>   But friend still walks by friend;
> No quarrels over ha'pence there
>   They pluck the trees for bread.

But the persistent refrain suggests that the speaker immediately sets aside Christian consolation and returns to
his lament: "What shall I do for pretty girls / Now my
old bawd is dead?" He apparently would prefer to live
with his "old bawd" than to pluck bread from the trees
in Eden. The "expectations" and the "pleasing habits"
he has referred to in this stanza almost surely have more
to do with the "old bawd" than would please a priest.
The power of the refrain shows that the Garden of Eden
serves merely as an analogy for expressing his lost
pleasures of bed and board and drinking with Mary
Moore.

"Man and the Echo"
(w. 1938, publ. 1939, *Poems* 345, *CP* 337)

Yeats's undiminished technical facility, evident in his use
of refrains, served him equally well in accomplishing the
lusty ends of "John Kinsella's Lament for Mrs. Mary
Moore" or in expressing an old man's unavoidable uncertainty as he nears death, in the quietly understated,

powerfully evocative dialogue of "Man and the Echo." This poem adroitly conveys what the man describes in the middle of the opening stanza:

> All that I have said and done,
> Now that I am old and ill,
> Turns into a question till
> I lie awake night after night
> And never get the answers right.

The "Echo," present even in the title of the poem, does more than simply echo the man's words. The pair of brief half lines that are spoken by the echo are so resonant that the poem is nearly a full-fledged dialogue: "Lie down and die" and "Into the night." The echo earns, by its dramatic force, the right to be addressed not as a mere echo but as "rocky voice," which comes from a cleft on the side of Ben Bulben.

The first echo, "Lie down and die," converts the man's simple declaration into an ominous imperative. In this poem, like "The Circus Animals' Desertion," which immediately follows in Yeats's arrangement, he thinks back over his career. He wonders if his fiercely patriotic play, *Cathleen ni Houlihan* (1902), contributed to the Easter Rising and its executions:

> Did that play of mine send out
> Certain men the English shot?

Then, remembering a more recent instance, he wonders if his words contributed to the mental breakdown of a young actress and poet, Margot Ruddock, in 1936:

> Did words of mine put too great strain
> On that woman's reeling brain?

This retrospective questioning is particularly appropriate to someone who is near death, for Yeats believed that a spirit's first task after death is to examine his or her own past by "tracing events to their sources," a process that is described in detail in the second stanza.[26]

The ominous echo at the end of the second stanza again has some imperative force and emphasizes the mysteriousness of death: "Into the night." The opening line of the final stanza repeats "night," but in an optimistic question: "Shall we in that great night rejoice?" Any thought of that possibility of joy disappears, together with workings of the spiritual intellect, at the terror-stricken death cry of a rabbit attacked by a predatory bird. Hawks and eagles, as in "An Acre of Grass," were among Yeats's favorite images of the strength and nobility of the mind. But here, as he faces death and the unknown, the mind's strength and nobleness are susceptible to a predator's attack: "A stricken rabbit is crying out, / And its cry distracts my thought." This painfully human and unheroic note of fear or uncertainty needs to be remembered equally with the confident bravura of his epitaph in "Under Ben Bulben"—"Cast a cold eye / On life, on death"— and the mixture of frivolity and regret in the final lines of "Politics"—"But O that I were young again / And held her in my arms." These contrasting responses to death enrich rather than cancel one another. "Man and the Echo" makes the courage of "Under Ben Bulben" all the more impressive, and both "Man and the Echo" and "Under Ben Bulben" sharpen the poignancy of "Politics" by their great distance from its casual tone.

"The Circus Animals' Desertion"
(w. 1937–38?, publ. 1939, *Poems* 346, *CP* 336)

"The Circus Animals' Desertion" contains within itself some of the contrasting attitudes about death of these late poems. Specifically, it confronts the loss—or apparent loss—of the poet's creative powers. Some readers find this poem to be a straightforward expression of artistic defeat by an old poet near death.[27] I prefer the opposite view that discovers a note of irony in the poet's assertion that he has lost his former ability to transform the materials of life into art.

Some evidence does suggest that "The Circus Animals' Desertion" could express sincere resignation to defeat. In the early drafts, Yeats considered titling the poem "Despair" or "On the Lack of a Theme."[28] And the opening stanza, with its treble repetition of the word "sought," enacts the poet's apparently fruitless searching for a theme: "I sought a theme and sought for it in vain, / I sought it daily for six weeks or so." That same opening stanza establishes the important and vivid antithesis between "my heart," which represents the poet's life, and "my circus animals," which are the creations of his art:

> Maybe at last being but a broken man
> I must be satisfied with my heart, although
> Winter and summer till old age began
> My circus animals were all on show.

Furthermore, breezily casual diction deflates his expected pride in his former artistic creations, the "circus animals": "Those stilted boys, that burnished chariot, / Lion and woman and the Lord knows what."

The three stanzas of the poem's central section rehearse those "old themes" in a tone that is more respectful, but that is still flavored by offhand touches in the second halves of several lines:

> sea-rider Oisin led by the nose
> . . . .
> Themes of the embittered heart, or so it seems
> . . . .
> Heart-mysteries there, and yet when all is said. . . .

These three stanzas together sketch an outline of Yeats's
artistic career, but at the same time each embodies a
larger contrast between art and life. The "allegorical
dreams" in *The Wanderings of Oisin* are balanced by the
poet's physical desires—"But what cared I that set him
on to ride, / I, starved for the bosom of his fairy bride."
In the next stanza the heroine of *The Countess Cathleen*
is paralleled with Maud Gonne and her devotion to Irish
nationalism. And in the last of those three stanzas the
characters of *On Baile's Strand* are set against the actual
"players and painted stage" that attracted so much of
Yeats's attention.

The poet says he is no longer able to produce the
"circus animals" of his art to put "on show" and therefore
that he must resign himself to be content with the ordinary stuff of life:

> A mound of refuse or the sweepings of a street,
> Old kettles, old bottles, and a broken can,
> Old iron, old bones, old rags. . . .

From these castoffs, his "pure mind" had formerly
created his circus animals. But now, the poet says, he
will have to be content with the impure things from
which art is made:

> Now that my ladder's gone
> I must lie down where all the ladders start
> In the foul rag and bone shop of the heart.

One important clue that these objects still do have worth
is that the "foul rag and bone shop" belongs to "the
heart." Thus, to move from "pure mind" to "the heart"
is not as catastrophic as the catalog of "refuse" might at
first suggest.

The problem for the reader is whether to take the
poet at his word or whether this poem uses the same

irony that had been employed in some earlier poems. The poet had said, in the opening section of "The Tower" (1925): "It seems that I must bid the Muse go pack." And before that, in 1908, he had insisted in "All Things can Tempt Me"—with equal irony—that he hoped to become "colder and dumber and deafer than a fish." I am persuaded that the poetic achievement of "The Circus Animals' Desertion" show him still in possession of his powers.

Yeats's last poems thus reflect his vigorous creative energy and the inexorable approach of death. He was capable of astonishing artistic achievement during his seventies, but he was not capable of warding off the decay of his body. Both the creative achievement and the bodily decay are subjects of "The Circus Animals' Desertion." But the poet's equation of "heart" with life testifies to his indefatigable willingness to accept life and to transform it into art. Even at the last, when he must look into the unignorable face of death, words still obey his call.

9

~~~~~~~~~~~~~~~~~~~~~~~~~~~~

Yeats and
Modern Poetry

Yeats, who numbered himself among "the last romantics," openly acknowledged the importance of his individual imagination and its power to transmute the
immediate circumstances of his life into art. Despite
the several radical changes in his poetic style during the
more than fifty years of his career, he remained unwavering in his allegiance to the Romantic poetical imagination.

His greatest poems articulate his personal percep-
tions, but enclose resonant truths that are never merely
personal and that are often too complex to be known with
certainty. He was unwilling to settle for simple answers,
and in the last month of his life could say, with considerable satisfaction: "I am happy, and I think full of an
energy. . . . It seems to me that I have found what I
wanted. When I try to put all into a phrase I say, 'Man
can embody truth but he cannot know it.' "[1] The embodiment was in his writing. The critic Balachandra Rajan
has tellingly observed that Yeats was able in his poems
to "drive an insight through against the derisions of irony
to a comprehension in which the attacking ironies are
included and transcended."[2] Those rhetorical accomplishments, together with his masterful powers of rhythm
and poetic phrase, have earned wide praise from his
readers and especially from his fellow poets.

Yeats's creative imagination remained very much his

own, isolated to a remarkable degree from the successive
fashions of modern poetry, despite his extensive contacts
with other poets. Yeats was in London for most of the
first three decades of his career, and especially during
the 1890s he knew many of the English poets of his
generation, such as Lionel Johnson, Robert Bridges and
John Masefield. He selected several contemporary poets
for publication by the Cuala Press, which was operated
by his sisters. Lecture tours in America and England and
the day-to-day management of the Abbey Theatre also
kept him in contact with contemporary writers. Ezra
Pound was a close friend in London from 1909 to 1918,
and later during Yeats's winters in Italy. The Nobel Prize
in 1923 gave him international attention. T. S. Eliot and
Yeats cooperated in the "Plays by Poets" series at the
Mercury Theatre, London, during the mid-1930s. And
he read widely in contemporary poetry while preparing
the *Oxford Book of Modern Verse*, published in 1936.
For all that, he remained essentially an outsider because
of his relentless concern for expressing the truth of his
individual imagination, because of his cultural allegiance
to Ireland, and to some extent because of his continuing
fascination with occultism.

Literary modernism held no inherent attraction for
Yeats except perhaps in its general association with youthful
vigor. He admired a wide range of traditional English
poetry and drama, as can be seen in his use of stanza
forms from the seventeenth century and in echoes of
phrases, such as the "topless towers" of Troy, in "Long-
legged Fly," taken from Christopher Marlowe's sixteenth-century play *The Tragical History of Dr. Faustus*.
Yeats was unconcerned that during the last two decades
of his life his preference for using rhyme and strict stanza
forms would set him apart from the vogue of modern
poetry. The extreme freedom of rhythm and diction of
Gerard Manley Hopkins, whose poems had not been
published until 1918, strongly impressed many poets in

the 1920s and afterwards. But the conservative Yeats ignored that fashion and publicly announced his dislike of those poems.[3] He was able to find vital, energetic poetic styles without turning his back on traditional metrical forms. Friendship with Ezra Pound, who led a loud campaign for extreme poetic modernism, never overturned Yeat's personal loyalty to the craftsmanship of rhyme and stanzas. Instead, Yeats took only what he found useful from Pound, notably an adaptation of Japanese Noh drama techniques, which helped to broaden the imaginative range of his plays.

Yeats's allegiance to poetic tradition did not extend, however, to what he considered an often obscure, overly learned use of literary and cultural traditions by T. S. Eliot and Pound. Yeats deplored the tremendous enthusiasm among younger poets for Eliot's "The Wasteland," published in 1922.[4] In a highly controversial introduction to the *Oxford Book of Modern Verse* Yeats complained that Eliot wrote "without apparent imagination" and with flat rhythms that could yield only a grey, cold, and dry mood.[5] Yeats insisted instead that all artistic work should be full of energy. The literary traditions that furnished Eliot with so many allusions and quotations should be included in a poem only if those traditions had so excited the poet's imagination that they could become poetic ingredients of the sort he described in "The Tower":

> Poet's imaginings
> And memories of love,
> Memories of the words of women.
> All those things whereof
> Man makes a superhuman
> Mirror-resembling dream.

Yeats wanted poetry to engage the full complexity of life, but only insofar as the individual poet's imagination had direct access to experience or thought, and only insofar as those materials were transformed by the energy of artistic articulation. Consequently he was un-impressed by the widely acclaimed pathos of Wilfred Owen and other World War I poets because, in Yeats's view, they had been content with passive presentation of suffering.[6]

When the reader turns from the opinions of Yeats about his fellow writers to their opinions of his work, it is discovered that the energy and intense dedication he required of his artistic expression—whether in poetry, drama, or prose—won him well-deserved admiration. Writers flattered him by imitation of his phrases, al-though during Yeats's lifetime those imitations often came only after he had already abandoned the poetic manner being imitated and had begun a new one. Recent book titles make such frequent use of phrases from Yeats that he is perhaps second only to Shakespeare as a source of inspiration for titles.

W. H. Auden, in an essay entitled "Yeats as an Example," published in 1948, suggested that he had learned much from Yeats and that he, like every young poet, inevitably began with an "excessive admiration" for "one or more of the mature poets of his time." He found Yeats exemplary both for having accepted the mod-ern necessity of having to make a lonely and deliberate "choice of the principles and presuppositions in terms of which he can make sense of his experience," and for continually extending his range of subjects and his poetic style. Auden particularly admired the success of Yeats in writing poems that have "the personal note of a man speaking about his personal friends in a particular set-ting" while giving those local materials a "symbolic public significance." Yeats's contribution to modern poetic style was to release "regular stanzaic poetry, whether reflec-tive or lyrical," from "iambic monotony." Auden was pleased that "in spite of all the rhythmical variations and the half-rhymes which provide freedom for the most natural and lucid speech, the formal base, i.e., the prosodic rhythms . . . and the rhyme patterns which supply coherent dignity and music, these remain audible." He assigned Yeats the high praise of having written "some of the most beautiful poetry" of his time and of having "rescued" English lyric poetry "from the dead hand of [the sixteenth-century poet Thomas] Campion and [the popular nineteenth-century Irish song writer] Tom Moore."[7]

Auden, Stephen Spender, and other poets of the 1930s generation were about twenty years old in 1928 when Yeats published *The Tower*, which Spender said, in a lecture published in 1965, was "the volume by a contemporary published in this century which most affected the style of other poets." Spender mentioned its immediate influence on W. H. Auden, Edith Sitwell, C. Day Lewis, Richard Eberhart, and himself, plus its later effect on Dylan Thomas, George Barker, Vernon Watkins, Theodore Roethke, and other poets, noting that Yeats "restored rhetoric to poetry," and "that a poet like Dylan Thomas would scarcely have been possible without him."[8] Spender, like other politically liberal poets of his generation, abominated many of the forthrightly reactionary values of Yeats, but admired the poems for their rhetorical power and their rhythms. He spoke of being "ravished" by the music of those poems—of having the lines of a poem permanently in his memory.[9] Similar testimony can be found later in a poem where the American poet Theodore Roethke announced, "I take this cadence from a man named Yeats"—and that Yeats's poetic rhythms "have tossed my heart and fiddled through my brain."[10] But Spender's highest praise went to Yeats for displaying an uncompromising sense of responsibility to his conscience and to art. The example of "Easter, 1916" helped Auden, Spender, and C. Day Lewis who, despite ferocious ideological antagonism to Yeats, expressed in their own poems the same complicated and severely qualified praise for the side they so strongly favored in the Spanish Civil War as had Yeats in describing the Easter Rising two decades earlier.[11]

Later generations of poets also have felt the influence of Yeats. The English poet Philip Larkin, who first read Yeats in 1943 while a university student, candidly recalled:

I spent the next three years trying to write like Yeats, not because I liked his personality or understood his ideas but out of infatuation with his music. . . . In fairness to myself, it must be admitted that it is a particularly potent music, pervasive as garlic.[12]

And Seamus Heaney, the prominent contemporary Irish poet, who was born in 1939, has pointed to Yeats's craftsmanship and dedication as exemplar influences on poets:

I admire the way that Yeats took on the world on his own terms, . . . the way he never accepted the terms of another's argument but propounded his own. I assume that this preemptoriness, this apparent arrogance, is exemplary in an artist, that it is proper and even necessary for him to insist on his own language, his own vision, his own terms of reference. . . . From an artist's point of view it is an act of integrity, or an act of cunning to protect the integrity.

Heaney, after acknowledging that "a very great poet can be a very bad influence on other poets," said that Yeats offers an example of labor and perseverance:

He is, indeed, the ideal example for a poet approaching middle age. He reminds you that revision and slog-work are what you may have to undergo if you seek the satisfaction of finish; he bothers you with the suggestion that if you have managed to do one kind of poem in your own way, you should cast off that way and face into another area of your experience until you have learned a new voice to say that area properly. He encourages you to experience a transfusion of energies from poetic forms themselves, reveals how the challenge of a metre can extend the resources of the voice. He proves that deliberation can be so intensified that it becomes synonymous with inspiration.[13]

Yeats's masterful command of language and his willingness to face squarely the full complexity of life have deservedly won him permanent fame. His accomplishments validate a pronouncement he made in 1885 in "The Song of the Happy Shepherd," the opening poem in his collected works: "Words alone are certain good."[14]

Notes

1. A Poet's Life

1. Told by Brinsely Macnamara on a BBC broadcast, June 1949, "W. B. Yeats: A Dublin Portrait" by William R. Rogers; rpt. in *In Excited Reverie: A Centenary Tribute to William Butler Yeats: 1865–1939*, ed. A. N. Jeffares and K. G. W. Cross (New York: Macmillan, 1965), p.3.
2. Edmund Dulac, "Without the Twilight," *The Arrow*, Summer 1939, p. 14.
3. Katharine Tynan, "William Butler Yeats," *Magazine of Poetry*, 1 (October 1889), 454; rpt. in *W. B. Yeats Letters to Katharine Tynan*, ed. Roger McHugh (Dublin: Clonmore and Reynolds, 1953), p. 174n.
4. Cornelius Weygandt, *On the Edge of Evening* (New York: Putnam's, 1946), p. 147; Jessie B. Rittenhouse, *My House of Life: An Autobiography* (Boston: Houghton Mifflin, 1934), p. 232; Shotaro Oshima, "An Interview with Mr. Junzo Sato," in *W. B. Yeats and Japan* (Tokyo: Hokuseido Press, 1965), p. 121; Stephen Spender, *World within World* (New York: Harcourt Brace, 1951), p. 148.
5. Padriac Colum, Thomas Davis lecture, Radio Eireann, in *The Yeats We Knew*, ed. Francis Macmanus (Cork: Mercier Press, 1965), p. 15. Alvin Langdon Coburn, *Alvin Langdon Coburn: Photographer: An Autobiography*, ed. Helmet and Alison Gernsheim (New York: Praeger, 1966), p. 70.
6. "Mac" [S. M. (Isa) Macnie] in 1923, quoted by Harold Speakman, *Here's Ireland* (New York: Dodd, Mead, 1927), p. 306. Edmund Dulac, "Without the Twilight," *The Arrow*, Summer 1939, p. 14.

7. *Letters to the New Island,* ed. Horace Reynolds (Cambridge: Harvard University Press, 1934), pp. 75–76.

8. (1895) *The Variorum Edition of the Poems of W. B. Yeats,* ed. Peter Allt and Russell K. Alspach (New York: Macmillan, 1957), p. 845.

9. (1908) *Variorum Poems,* pp. 843–44.

10. Trans. E. B. Pusey, quoted by Richard J. Finneran (ed.), *The Poems: A New Edition,* by W. B. Yeats (New York: Macmillan, 1983), p. 619.

11. *Uncollected Prose by W. B. Yeats,* ed. John P. Frayne and Colton Johnson (New York: Columbia University Press, 1970 and 1976), I, 248.

12. *Uncollected Prose,* I, 250.

13. *Uncollected Prose,* I, 274.

14. W. B. Yeats, *Is the Order of R. R. & A. C. to remain a Magical Order?* (Privately printed, 1901), pp. 7–8.

15. *Essays and Introductions* (London: Macmillan, 1961), pp. 287–88.

16. W. B. Yeats, *Memoirs: Autobiography—First Draft, Journal,* ed. Denis Donoghue (London: Macmillan, 1972), p. 225.

17. (w. 1912, publ. 1914), W. B. Yeats, *The Poems: A New Edition,* ed. Richard J. Finneran (New York: Macmillan, 1983), p. 127; *The Collected Poems of W. B. Yeats* (London: Macmillan, 1950), p. 125.

18. (1922) *The Letters of W. B. Yeats,* ed. Allan Wade (London: Macmillan, 1954), p. 693.

19. *Letters,* p. 745.

20. W. B. Yeats, speech reported in the *Irish Times,* 18 February 1933, quoted by Donald T. Torchiana, *W. B. Yeats & Georgian Ireland* (Evanston: Northwestern University Press, 1966), p. 102.

21. Ibid.

2. BACKGROUNDS FOR READING YEATS'S POEMS

1. Information from Mrs. Yeats, in Curtis B. Bradford, "George Yeats: Poet's Wife," *Sewanee Review,* 77 (1969), 398.

2. *A Critical Edition of Yeats's A Vision (1925)*, ed. George
    M. Harper and Walter K. Hood (London: Macmillan,
    1978), p. 21 (note to p. 75, line 10).
3. W. B. Yeats, *Mythologies* (London: Macmillan, 1959),
    p. 334.
4. "All Things can tempt Me"; my italics.
5. *Variorum Poems*, p. 174.
6. For simplicity in the discussion I have ignored two spell-
    ing changes, neither of which probably is authorial, in
    The Celtic Twilight (1902): "hight" (a printer's error) and
    "whimsy" (an acceptable variant spelling).
7. *The Variorum Edition of the Poems of W. B. Yeats*, ed.
    Peter Allt and Russell K. Alspach (New York: Macmillan,
    1957); for the few additional poems that were published
    in Yeats's plays, see *The Variorum Edition of the Plays
    of W. B. Yeats*, ed. Russell K. Alspach (New York: Mac-
    millan, 1966).

3. THE EARLY POEMS

1. (1892 only) *Poems*, p. 619.
2. *Poems*, p. 589.
3. *Variorum Poems*, p. 103.
4. (1917) *Mythologies*, pp. 356–57.
5. In all versions until 1925 this phrase was "small slate-
    coloured bag." *Variorum Poems*, p. 104.
6. (1892 only) *Variorum Poems*, p. 104.
7. (1888) *Letters*, pp. 99–100. For the influence of Thoreau's
    Walden, see W. B. Yeats, *Autobiographies* (London:
    Macmillan, 1955), pp. 71–72; for the poem's backgrounds
    in legend, see Warwick Gould, "Yeats as Aborigine," *Four
    Decades of Poetry: 1890–1930*, 2 (1978), 65–76.
8. (1899 only) *Variorum Poems*, p. 803.
9. Allen R. Grossman, *Poetic Knowledge in the Early Yeats:
    A Study of The Wind among the Reeds* (Charlottesville:
    University Press of Virginia, 1969), pp. 106–09.
10. *Variorum Poems*, p. 800.
11. Fiona MacLeod [William Sharp], "A Group of Celtic
    Writers," *Fortnightly Review*, 1 January 1899; rpt. in

W. B. Yeats: The Critical Heritage, ed. A. Norman Jeffares (London: Routledge & Kegan Paul, 1977), p. 101.

12. (1908) *Variorum Poems*, p. 800.

4. THE NEW STYLE: 1900–1914

1. *The Oxford Book of Modern Verse: 1892–1935*, ed. W. B. Yeats (Oxford: Clarendon Press, 1936), p. xi.
2. Maud Gonne MacBride, *A Servant of the Queen: Reminiscences* (London: Gollancz, 1938), pp. 328–30; see also Joseph Hone, *W. B. Yeats: 1865–1939*, 2nd ed. (London: Macmillan, 1965), pp. 156–57.
3. (1909) *Memoirs*, p. 229.
4. "The Ballad of Moll Magee" and "The Ballad of the Foxhunter," *Poems*, p. 24–25.
5. *Poems*, p. 593.
6. *Letters*, p. 876.
7. *Poems*, pp. 593–94.
8. (1907) W. B. Yeats, *Essays and Introductions*, p. 246.
9. Maud Gonne MacBride, "Yeats and Ireland," in *Scattering Branches: Tributes to the Memory of W. B. Yeats*, ed. Stephen Gwynn (London: Macmillan, 1940), p. 31.
10. F. S. L. Lyons, *Charles Stewart Parnell* (New York: Oxford University Press, 1977), p. 128 and a photo between pp. 176–77.
11. Maud Gonne MacBride, "Yeats and Ireland," in *Scattering Branches*, ed. Gwynn, p. 17: ". . . masses of gold-brown hair." See also Marie nic Shiubhlaigh, *The Splendid Years* (Dublin: Duffy, 1955), p. 19: ". . . Maud Gonne, her rich golden hair."
12. Maud Gonne MacBride, "Yeats and Ireland," in *Scattering Branches*, ed. Gwynn, p. 17.
13. Nic Shiubhlaigh, *Splendid Years*, p. 19.
14. *Essays and Introductions*, p. 249.

5. NEW THOUGHTS: 1915–1921

1. W. B. Yeats, *Autobiographies*, p. 464.
2. M. H. Abrams, "Structure and Style in the Greater Ro-

mantic Lyric," *From Sensibility to Romanticism: Essays Presented to Frederick A. Pottle,* ed. Frederick W. Hilles and Harold Bloom (New York: Oxford University Press, 1965), pp. 527–60.

3. Painting in the collection of Miss Anne Yeats. George Moore, *Hail and Farewell: I: Ave* (London: Heinemann, 1911), pp. 246–47.

4. A. Norman Jeffares, *A Commentary on the Collected Poems of W. B. Yeats* (Stanford: Stanford University Press,1968) p. 155.

5. Jeffares, *Commentary,* p. 154.

6. William Rothenstein, *Men and Memories: Recollections of William Rothenstein* (New York: Coward-McCann, 1932), II, 321.

7. Hone, *W. B. Yeats,* p. 299.

8. *Letters,* p. 613.

9. Ibid., p. 613.

10. Ibid., p. 614.

11. Ibid., p. 614.

12. Maud Gonne MacBride, "Yeats and Ireland," in *Scattering Branches,* ed. Gwynn, pp. 30–31; she mistakenly recalled the month as September.

13. Quoted in John Eglinton [William Kirkpatrick Magee], *A Memoir of George Russell* (London: Macmillan, 1937), pp. 119–20 and *1000 Years of Irish Poetry,* ed. Kathleen Hoagland (1947; rpt. New York: Grosset & Dunlap, 1962), pp. 616–17.

14. *Essays and Introductions,* pp. 313–14.

15. For a careful study of the drafts, see Stallworthy, *Between the Lines,* pp. 16–25.

16. Ibid., pp. 17–21.

17. Richard Ellmann, *The Identity of Yeats,* 2nd ed. (London: Faber, 1964), p. 290.

18. *Poems,* pp. 646–48.

19. Stallworthy, *Between the Lines,* pp. 32–33, 24–25.

6. POEMS 1922–1926

1. (1927) *Poems,* p. 595.

2. Unpublished note that Yeats wrote for a radio broadcast

but did not use, quoted by Stallworthy, *Between the Lines,*
pp. 96–97.

3. *A Vision* (1925), p. 191; also in *A Vision* (1937), p. 279.
4. *A Vision* (1925), pp. 191–92; also in *A Vision* (1937), pp. 280–81.
5. Length 5 5 5 4 5 4 4 5; rhymed *aabbcddc.*
6. *A Vision* (1925), p. 181; also in *A Vision* (1937), p. 268.
7. Ellmann, *Identity of Yeats,* pp. 177–78.
8. Donald T. Torchiana, " 'Among School Children' and the Education of the Irish Spirit," in *In Excited Reverie,* ed. Jeffares and Cross, p. 123.
9. (1927) *Poems* , p. 597.
10. Walter Burkert, *Lore and Science in Ancient Pythagoreanism,* trans. Edwin L. Minar, Jr. (Cambridge: Harvard University Press, 1972), pp. 141–43, 159–61, 488–92.

7. POEMS 1927–1935

1. (1927) *Letters,* p. 729.
2. Titled "Coole Park and Ballylee, 1931" in *Collected Poems.*
3. Quoted by Hone, *W. B. Yeats,* p. 425.
4. Unpublished manuscript quoted by Thomas Parkinson, *W. B. Yeats: The Later Poems* (Berkeley and Los Angeles: University of California Press, 1966), p. 143.
5. Another local stream ends at a swallow hole much closer to the spring that feeds Coole River, but the swallow hole near Thoor Ballylee has an advantage of twenty feet higher elevation.
6. Sale catalog, 8–9 August 1932; "Low Prices at Gort Sale," *The Irish Press,* 10 August 1932, p. 2, col. 5; and "Lady Gregory's Furniture," *The Irish Times,* 10 August 1932, p. 4, col. 5.
7. Stallworthy, *Between the Lines,* p. 136.
8. *A Vision* (1925), p. 193; also in *A Vision* (1937), pp. 281–82.
9. *A Vision* (1925), p. 191; also in *A Vision* (1937), p. 279.
10. (1930) W. B. Yeats, *Explorations* (London: Macmillan, 1962), p. 290; the difference was first pointed out by

Frederick L. Gwynn, "Yeats's Byzantium and Its Sources," *Philological Quarterly*, 32 (1953), 9–21.

11. *A Vision* (1925), p. 194; also in *A Vision* (1937), p. 283.
12. (1930) *Explorations*, p. 290.
13. "Modern Ireland: An Address to American Audiences: 1932–1933," ed. Curtis Bradford, *The Massachusetts Review*, 5 (Winter 1964), 262n.
14. In this I follow the example of T. R. Henn, whose lucid analysis of the poem is found in *The Lonely Tower: Studies in the Poetry of W. B. Yeats*, 2nd ed. (London: Methuen, 1965), pp. 228–37.
15. For a useful and brief overview of this position see Richard J. Finneran, Introduction, *The Byzantium Poems*, Literary Casebook series (Columbus, OH: Merrill, 1970), pp. 1–10.
16. Ellmann, *Identity of Yeats*, pp. 219–22. Helen Vendler, *Yeats's Vision and the Later Plays* (Cambridge: Harvard University Press, 1963), pp. 114–18.
17. *Poems*, p. 598. The prose draft of "Byzantium" is dated 30 April 1930; he finished the poem in September 1930.
18. Ibid., p. 598.
19. (1933) *Letters*, p. 814.
20. (1931) *Letters*, pp. 785–86.
21. *The Variorum Edition of the Plays of W. B. Yeats*, ed. Russell K. Alspach (New York: Macmillan, 1966), pp. 254, 239 and *Poems*, p. 540.
22. Ole Munch-Pederson, in "Crazy Jane: A Cycle of Popular Literature," *Eire-Ireland*, 14 (1979), 56–59, suggests that Yeats found her new name in a popular nineteenth-century ballad about Crazy Jane, a girl who was deserted by her lover.
23. Quoted by Hone, *W. B. Yeats*, p. 425.
24. Ellmann, *Identity of Yeats*, p. 275.

8. AN OLD MAN'S EAGLE MIND: 1936–1939

1. *Letters*, p. 838.
2. *Essays and Introductions*, p. 437.
3. *Explorations*, p. 170.

4. (1910) *Essays and Introductions*, p. 243.
5. *Essays and Introductions*, pp. 522–23.
6. *Explorations*, pp 448–49.
7. Ellmann, *Identity of Yeats*, pp. 185–87.
8. *Letters*, p. 837.
9. See "An Indian Monk" (1932) and "The Holy Mountain" (1934), *Essays and Introductions*, pp. 427, 466–67, 471 and *A Vision* (1937), p. 257.
10. *Oxford Book of Modern Verse*, p. xxxiv.
11. (1916) *Essays and Introductions*, p. 225. *A Vision* (1925), p. 183; also in *A Vision* (1937), p. 270. For the art-historical backgrounds to this poem, see my essay "The Art of Yeats's 'Lapis Lazulis,' " *The Massachusetts Review*, 23 (1982), 353–67.
12. *Essays and Introductions*, p. 225.
13. Shakespeare, *Timon of Athens*, V, iv, 72–73.
14. "Samhain 1904," *Explorations*, p. 163; see also "Poetry and Tradition" (1907), *Essays and Introductions*, p. 255.
15. Spoken by the autobiographical hero in Yeats's unfinished novel in 1902, *The Speckled Bird*, ed. W. H. O'Donnell (Toronto: McClelland and Stewart, 1977), p. 43.
16. Introduction, *The Poems of William Blake*, 2nd ed. (London: Routledge, 1905), p. xvii.
17. *A Vision* (1925), p. 183; also in *A Vision* (1937), p. 271.
18. *Variorum Poems*, p. 837.
19. Richard J. Finneran, *Editing Yeats's Poems* (London: Macmillan, 1983), p. 65.
20. Jon Stallworthy, *Vision and Revision in Yeats's Last Poems* (Oxford: Clarendon Press, 1969), pp. 148–49.
21. Hone, *W. B. Yeats*, p. 477.
22. *Oxford Book of Modern Verse*, pp. xxiv–xxv.
23. *The Collected Plays of W. B. Yeats* (London: Macmillan, 1952), p. 587; also in *Poems*, p. 567 (as "[Astrea's holy child].").
24. Interview with Bernard Price in "Yeats in Sussex," BBC, broadcast 4 September 1966, quoted by Stallworthy, *Vision and Revision*, p. 115.
25. *Letters*, p. 912.
26. (1934), *Explorations*, p. 366 and *Variorum Plays*, pp. 968–69. See also "Shepherd and Goatherd" (1918), lines 89–

112, *Poems* pp. 144–45, and Yeats's note to *The Dreaming of the Bones* (1923), *Variorum Poems*, pp. 777–78.

27. For example, Stanley Sultan, *Yeats at His Last* (Dublin: Dolmen, 1975), pp. 42–43.

28. Curtis Bradford, *Yeats at Work* (Carbondale: Southern Illinois University Press, 1965), p. 164.

9. Yeats and Modern Poetry

1. Yeats letter to Lady Elizabeth Pelham, 4 January 1939, quoted by Hone, *W. B. Yeats*, p. 476.

2. Balachandra Rajan, *W. B. Yeats: A Critical Introduction*, 2nd ed. (London: Hutchinson, 1969), p. 190.

3. *Oxford Book of Modern Verse*, pp. xxxix–xl.

4. (1935), *Letters*, p. 833.

5. *Oxford Book of Modern Verse*, p. xxi.

6. Ibid., pp. xxxiv–xxxv.

7. W. H. Auden, "Yeats as an Example," *The Kenyon Review*, 10 (1948), 187, 192–95.

8. Stephen Spender, "The Influence of Yeats on Later English Poets," *Tri-Quarterly*, 4 (Winter 1965), 85.

9. Ibid., p. 86.

10. "The Dance" (1952), in "Four for Sir John Davies," *The Collected Poems of Theodore Roethke* (Garden City, NY: Doubleday, 1966), p. 105.

11. Ibid., pp. 87–89.

12. Philip Larkin, Introduction, *The North Ship*, 2nd ed. (London: Faber, 1966), p. 9.

13. Seamus Heaney, "Yeats as an Example?" (1978 lecture), *Preoccupations: Selected Prose 1968–1978* (London: Faber, 1980), pp. 101, 109–10.

14. *Poems*, p. 8, l. 43.

Bibliography

1. Works by William Butler Yeats

Poetry

The Wanderings of Oisin and Other Poems. London: Kegan Paul, Trench, 1889.

The Countess Kathleen and Various Legends and Lyrics. London: Unwin, 1892.

Poems. London: Unwin, 1895.

The Wind among the Reeds. London: Mathews, 1899.

In the Seven Woods. Dundrum, Co. Dublin: Dun Emer Press, 1903.

The Green Helmet and Other Poems. Dundrum: Cuala Press, 1910.

Poems Written in Discouragement: 1912–1913. Dundrum: Cuala Press, 1913,

Responsibilities. Dundrum: Cuala Press, 1914.

The Wild Swans at Coole. Dundrum: Cuala Press, 1917; enlarged edition, London: Macmillan, 1919.

Michael Robartes and the Dancer. Dundrum: Cuala Press, 1921 (title page: 1920).

The Cat and the Moon and Certain Poems. Dublin: Cuala Press, 1924.

October Blast. Dublin: Cuala Press, 1927.

The Tower. London: Macmillan, 1928.

The Winding Stair. New York: Fountain Press, 1929; enlarged edition, London: Macmillan, 1933.

Words for Music Perhaps and Other Poems. Dublin: Cuala Press, 1932.

A Full Moon in March. London: Macmillan, 1935.

New Poems. Dublin: Cuala Press, 1938.

Last Poems and Two Plays. Dublin: Cuala Press, 1939.

Poems. 2 vols. London: Macmillan, 1949.

The Collected Poems of W. B. Yeats. London: Macmillan, 1950.

The Variorum Edition of the Poems of W. B. Yeats. Ed. Peter Allt and Russell K. Alspach. New York: Macmillan, 1957. (Texts of all published versions.)

The Poems: A New Edition. Ed. Richard J. Finneran. New York: Macmillan, 1983. (First volume of the Macmillan Edition of W. B. Yeats; reliable text of all the poems; explanatory notes.)

Plays

The Countess Cathleen. In *The Countess Kathleen and Various Legends and Lyrics.* London: Unwin, 1892. (Performed 1899.)

The Land of Heart's Desire. London: Unwin, 1894. (Performed 1894.)

The Shadowy Waters. London: Hodder and Stoughton, 1900. (Performed 1904.)

Cathleen ni Houlihan. London: Bullen, 1902. (Performed 1902.)

On Baile's Strand. In *In the Seven Woods.* Dundrum, Co. Dublin: Dun Emer Press, 1903. (Performed 1904.)

The Hour-Glass. London: Heinemann, 1903. (Performed 1903.)

The Pot of Broth. In *The Hour-Glass and Other Plays.* New York: Macmillan, 1904. (Performed 1902.)

The King's Threshold. New York: Privately printed, 1904. (Performed 1903.)

Deirdre. London: Bullen, 1907. (Performed 1906.)

The Unicorn from the Stars. (By W. B. Yeats and Lady Gregory.) New York: Macmillan, 1908. (Performed 1907.) Revised from *Where There is Nothing.* (By W. B. Yeats.) London: Lane, 1902. (Performed 1904.)

The Green Helmet. In *The Green Helmet and Other Poems.* Dundrum: Cuala Press, 1910. (Performed 1910.) Revised from *The Golden Helmet.* New York: John Quinn, 1908. (Performed 1908.)

At the Hawk's Well. In *The Wild Swans at Coole, Other Verses and a Play.* Dundrum: Cuala Press, 1917. (Performed 1916.)

The Dreaming of the Bones. In *Two Plays for Dancers.* Dundrum: Cuala Press, 1919. (Performed 1931.)

The Only Jealousy of Emer. In *Two Plays for Dancers.* Dundrum: Cuala Press, 1919. (Performed 1926.) Rewritten as *Fighting the Waves.* In *Wheels and Butterflies.* London: Macmillan, 1934. (Performed 1929.)

Calvary. In *Four Plays for Dancers.* London: Macmillan, 1921.

The Player Queen. In *Plays in Prose and Verse.* London: Macmillan, 1922. (Performed 1919.)

The Cat and the Moon. In *The Cat and the Moon and Certain Poems.* Dublin: Cuala Press, 1924. (Performed 1926.)

Sophocles' King Oedipus. London: Macmillan, 1928. (Performed 1926.)

The Resurrection. In *Stories of Michael Robartes and his Friends.* Dublin: Cuala Press, 1932 (title page: 1931). (Performed 1934.)

The Words upon the Window-Pane. Dublin: Cuala Press, 1934. (Performed 1930.)

Sophocles' Oedipus at Colonus. In *The Collected Plays of W. B. Yeats.* London: Macmillan, 1934. (Performed 1927.)

The King of the Great Clock Tower. Dublin: Cuala Press, 1934. (Performed 1934.)

A Full Moon in March. London: Macmillan, 1935. (Performed 1950.)

The Herne's Egg. London: Macmillan, 1935. (Performed 1950.)

Purgatory. In *Last Poems and Two Plays.* Dublin: Cuala Press, 1939. (Performed 1938.)

The Death of Cuchulain. In *Last Poems and Two Plays.* Dublin: Cuala Press, 1939. (Performed 1949.)

Diamuid and Grania (By W. B. Yeats and George Moore.) Dublin: Becker, 1951. (Performed 1901.)

The Collected Plays of W. B. Yeats. London: Macmillan, 1952.

The Variorum Edition of the Plays of W. B. Yeats. Ed. Russell K. Alspach. New York: Macmillan, 1966. (Texts of all published versions.)

Prose: Autobiographies and Diaries

Reveries over Childhood and Youth. Dundrum, Co. Dublin:
    Cuala Press, 1916 (title page: 1915).
Four Years. Dundrum: Cuala Press, 1921.
The Trembling of the Veil. London: T. Werner Laurie (by
    subscription), 1922.
The Death of Synge and other Passages from an old Diary.
    Dublin: Cuala Press, 1928.
Dramatis Personae. Dublin: Cuala Press, 1935.
Pages from a Diary Written in Nineteen Hundred and Thirty.
    Dublin: Cuala Press, 1944.
Autobiographies. (Collected edition.) London: Macmillan, 1955.
Memoirs: Autobiography—First Draft, Journal. Ed. Denis
    Donoghue. London: Macmillan, 1972.

Prose: Essays

The Celtic Twilight. London: Lawrence and Bullen, 1893; en-
    larged edition. London: Bullen, 1902.
Ideas of Good and Evil. London: Bullen, 1903.
Discoveries. Dundrum, Co. Dublin: Dun Emer Press, 1907.
The Cutting of an Agate. New York: Macmillan, 1912; enlarged
    edition, London: Macmillan, 1919.
Per Amica Silentia Lunae. London: Macmillan, 1918.
Plays and Controversies. London: Macmillan, 1923.
The Bounty of Sweden. Dublin: Cuala Press, 1925.
A Vision. London: T. Werner Laurie (by subscription), 1925
    (issued 1926); revised edition, London: Macmillan, 1937.
A Packet for Ezra Pound. Dublin: Cuala Press, 1929.
Letters to the New Island. (Reviews and essays published in
    American newspapers, 1888–1892.) Ed. Horace Reynolds.
    Cambridge: Harvard University Press, 1934.
Essays: 1931 to 1936. Dublin: Cuala Press, 1937.
On the Boiler. Dublin: Cuala Press, 1939.
If I were Four-and-Twenty. Dublin: Cuala Press, 1940.
The Senate Speeches of W. B. Yeats. Ed. Donald R. Pearce.
    Bloomington: Indiana University Press, 1960.
Essays and Introductions. London: Macmillan, 1961.
Explorations. (Additional essays and introductions.) Selected
    by Mrs. W. B. Yeats. London: Macmillan, 1962.

Uncollected Prose by W. B. Yeats. Ed. John P. Frayne and Colton Johnson. 2 vols. New York: Columbia University Press, 1970 and 1976.

Prose: Fiction

John Sherman and Dhoya. London: Unwin, 1891.
The Secret Rose. London: Lawrence & Bullen, 1897.
The Tables of the Law. The Adoration of the Magi. London: "Privately printed" [Lawrence & Bullen], 1897.
Stories of Red Hanrahan. Dundrum, Co. Dublin: Dun Emer Press, 1905 (title page: 1904).
Stories of Michael Robartes and his Friends. Dublin: Cuala Press, 1932 (title page: 1931).
Mythologies. (Collected stories and some essays.) London: Macmillan, 1959.
The Speckled Bird. (Unfinished novel.) Ed. William H. O'Donnell. Dublin: Cuala Press, 1974; annotated edition, Toronto: McClelland and Stewart, 1977 (title page: 1976).
The Secret Rose: Stories by W. B. Yeats: A Variorum Edition. Ed. Phillip L. Marcus, Warwick Gould, and Michael J. Sidnell. Ithaca: Cornell University Press, 1981. (Texts of all published versions.)

Letters

The Collected Letters of W. B. Yeats: Volume One: 1865–1895. Ed. John Kelly and Eric Domville. Oxford: Clarendon Press, 1986.
J. B. Yeats: Letters to His Son W. B. Yeats and Others: 1869–1922. Ed. Joseph Hone. London: Faber, 1944.
The Letters of W. B. Yeats. Ed. Allan Wade. London: Macmillan, 1954. (Recommended.)
Letters on Poetry from W. B. Yeats to Dorothy Wellesley. London: Oxford University Press, 1940.
Letters to W. B. Yeats. Ed. Richard J. Finneran, George M. Harper, and William M. Murphy. 2 vols. London: Macmillan, 1977.
Theatre Business: The Correspondence of the First Abbey Theatre Directors: William Butler Yeats, Lady Gregory and J.

M. Synge. Ed. Ann Saddlemyer. Gerrards Cross, Bucks.: Colin Smythe, 1982.

W. B. Yeats and T. Sturge Moore: Their Correspondence: 1901–1937. Ed. Ursula Bridge. London: Routledge & Kegan Paul, 1953.

2. Works about William Butler Yeats

Bibliography of Works by Yeats

Wade, Allan. *A Bibliography of the Writings of W. B. Yeats.* 3rd. ed. rev. Russell K. Alspach. London: Hart-Davis, 1968. (A 4th edition, edited by Colin Smythe, is in preparation.)

Bibliographies of Works about Yeats

Jochum, K. P. S. *W. B. Yeats: A Classified Bibliography of Criticism.* Urbana: University of Illinois Press, 1978. (This standard work gives thorough coverage of works about Yeats through 1971 and with some works to 1973.)

Finneran, Richard J. "W. B. Yeats" in *Anglo-Irish Literature: A Review of Research.* New York: Modern Language Association, 1976 and in *Recent Research on Anglo-Irish Writers.* New York: Modern Language Association, 1983. (Comprehensive review essays through 1980 and part of 1981.)

Jochum, K. P. S. Annual Bibliography of Yeats Criticism (1981–) in *Yeats: An Annual of Critical and Textual Studies.* Ithaca: Cornell University Press, 1983–.

Gould, Warwick and Olympia Sitwell. Yeats Bibliography (1981–) in *Yeats Annual.* No. 3 –. London: Macmillan, 1985 –.

Concordances

Parrish, Steven M. *A Concordance to the Poems of W. B. Yeats.* Ithaca: Cornell University Press, 1963.

Domville, Eric. *A Concordance to the Plays of W. B. Yeats.* 2 vols. Ithaca: Cornell University Press, 1972.

Handbooks

Jeffares, A. Norman. *A New Commentary on the Poems of W. B. Yeats*. Stanford: Stanford University Press, 1984. (Recommended)

———. and A. S. Knowland. *A Commentary on the Collected Plays of W. B. Yeats*. London: Macmillan, 1975.

Kirby, Sheelah. *The Yeats Country*. 3rd ed. Dublin: Dolmen, 1969. (Brief introduction to Yeats's geographical references to the West of Ireland.)

McGarry, James. *Place Names in the Writings of William Butler Yeats*. Gerrards Cross Bucks.: Colin Smythe, 1976. (Reliable.)

The Macmillan Dictionary of Irish Literature. Ed. Robert Hogan. London: Macmillan, 1979. (Reliable.)

Malins, Edward. *A Preface to Yeats*. Preface Books series. London: Longman, 1974. (Brief, moderately useful miscellany of background topics; discussions of a few poems.)

Unterecker, John. *A Reader's Guide to William Butler Yeats*. New York: Noonday Press, 1959. (Detailed readings of many poems and discussions of major themes.)

Introductory Studies

Bradley, Anthony. *William Butler Yeats*. Literature and Life series. New York: Ungar, 1979. (Good introductions to each of the plays and helpful background information, including a survey of Irish legends and history; a companion volume to this book; recommended.)

Cowell, Raymond. *W. B. Yeats*. Literature in Perspective series. London: Evans, 1969. (Brief, straightforward survey of poetry, plays, and life.)

Peterson, Richard. *William Butler Yeats*. English Authors series. Boston: Twayne, 1982. (Useful survey of poetry, plays, and life.)

Rajan, Balachandra. *W. B. Yeats: A Critical Introduction*. London: Hutchinson, 1965. (Able survey of the poetry and plays.)

Stock, Amy G. *W. B. Yeats: His Poetry and Thought*. Cambridge: Cambridge University Press, 1961. (Introductory survey emphasizing the Irish background and *A Vision*.)

Biographies

Ellmann, Richard. *Yeats: The Man and the Masks.* 2nd ed. London: Faber, 1961. (Brief, tightly unified critical biography; full of excellent insights; recommended.)

Hone, Joseph W. *W. B. Yeats: 1865–1939.* 2nd ed. London: Macmillan, 1965. (Fullest available biography.)

Jeffares, A. Norman. *W. B. Yeats: Man and Poet.* 2nd ed. New York: Barnes and Noble, 1966. (Useful exposition of backgrounds; recommended.)

MacLiammóir, Micheál and Eavan Boland. *W. B. Yeats and his world.* London: Thames and Hudson, 1971. (Pictorial biography.)

Tuohy, Frank. *Yeats.* New York: Macmillan, 1976. (Brief, well illustrated biography.)

General Studies

Archibald, Douglas. *Yeats.* Syracuse: Syracuse University Press, 1983. (General survey concentrating on influences.)

Bloom, Harold. *Yeats.* New York: Oxford University Press, 1970. (Controversial, very rapid survey of Yeats as a writer in the romantic tradition.)

Donoghue, Denis. *William Butler Yeats.* Modern Masters series. New York: Viking, 1971. (Interesting introductory study of Yeats's search for power.)

Ellmann, Richard. *The Identity of Yeats.* 2nd ed. London: Faber, 1964. (Emphasizes the consistency of language, imagery, and thought in Yeats's career; recommended.)

Henn, Thomas R. *The Lonely Tower.* 2nd ed. London: Methuen, 1965. (Good on the Anglo-Irish background, *A Vision,* and the visual arts; recommended.)

Specialized Studies (Manuscripts and Revisions)

Bradford, Curtis B. *Yeats at Work.* Carbondale: Southern Illinois University Press, 1965. (Poetry, plays, and prose.)

———. "Yeats's Byzantium Poems: A Study of their Development." *PMLA*, 75 (1960), 110–25.

Clark, David R. *Yeats at Songs and Choruses.* Amherst: University of Massachusetts Press, 1983. ("After Long Silence,"

"Crazy Jane on the Day of Judgment," "Colonus' Praise," "From 'Oedipus at Colonus,' " "From the 'Antigone,' " "Her Triumph," "Michael Robartes and the Dancer," and "Three Things.")

Parkinson, Thomas. *W. B. Yeats: Self-Critic: A Study of his Early Verse* and *W. B. Yeats: The Later Poetry.* 1951 and 1964; rpt. in one volume, Berkeley and Los Angeles: University of California Press, 1971. (Excellent study of Yeats's style.)

Stallworthy, Jon. *Between the Lines: Yeats's Poetry in the Making.* Oxford: Clarendon Press, 1963. ("An Acre of Grass," "After Long Silence," "The Black Tower," "A Bronze Head," "Byzantium," "Chosen: Parting," "Consolation," "Coole Park, 1929," "The Gift of Harun Al-Rashid," "The Nineteenth Century and After," "In Memory of Eva Gore-Booth and Con Markiewicz," "Memory," "A Prayer for my Daughter," "Sailing to Byzantium," "The Second Coming," "The Sorrow of Love"; recommended.)

——. *Vision and Revision in Yeats's Last Poems.* Oxford: Clarendon Press, 1969. ("The Lady . . . and the Chambermaid" series, "Lapis Lazuli," "Long-legged Fly," "The Man and the Echo," "The Spur," "The Statues," "The Three Bushes," "Under Ben Bulben"; recommended.)

Other Specialized Studies of Yeats's Poems

Adams, Hazard. *Blake and Yeats: The Contrary Vision.* Ithaca: Cornell University Press, 1955.

Albright, Daniel. *The Myth against Myth: A Study of Yeats's Imagination in Old Age.* London: Oxford University Press, 1972.

Bohlmann, Otto. *Yeats and Nietzsche: An Exploration of Major Nietzchean Echoes in the Writings of William Butler Yeats.* London: Macmillan, 1982.

Brown, Malcolm. *The Politics of Irish Literature: From Thomas Davis to W. B. Yeats.* Seattle: University of Washington Press, 1972.

Cullingford, Elizabeth. *Yeats, Ireland and Fascism.* New York: New York University Press, 1982.

Desai, Rupin. *Yeats's Shakespeare*. Evanston: Northwestern University Press, 1971.

Engelberg, Edward. *The Vast Design: Patterns in W. B. Yeats's Aesthetic*. Toronto: University of Toronto Press, 1964.

Finneran, Richard J., ed. *Critical Essays on W. B. Yeats*. Boston: G. K. Hall, 1986.

Freyer, Grattan. *W. B. Yeats and the Anti-Democratic Tradition*. Dublin: Gill and Macmillan, 1981. (Political backgrounds.)

Garab, Arra. *Beyond Byzantium: The Last Phase of Yeats's Career*. DeKalb: Northern Illinois University Press, 1964.

Grossman, Allen. *Poetic Knowledge in the Early Yeats: A Study of The Wind among the Reeds*. Charlottesville: University Press of Virginia, 1969.

Marcus, Phillip. *Yeats and the Beginning of the Irish Renaissance*. Ithaca: Cornell University Press, 1970. (Nineteenth-century Irish literary background.)

Moore, Virginia. *The Unicorn: Yeats's Search for Reality*. New York: Macmillan, 1954. (The occult.)

Olney, James. *The Rhizome and the Flower: The Perennial Philosophy—Yeats and Jung*. Berkeley and Los Angeles: University of California Press, 1980.

Snuknal, Robert. *High Talk: The Philosophical Poetry of W. B. Yeats*. New York: Cambridge University Press, 1973. (Yeats and Immanuel Kant.)

Thurley, Geoffrey. *The Turbulent Dream: Passion and Politics in the Poetry of W. B. Yeats*. St. Lucia: University of Queensland Press, 1983.

Torchiana, Donald. *W. B. Yeats and Georgian Ireland*. Evanston: Northwestern University Press, 1966.

Whitaker, Thomas. *Swan and Shadow: Yeats's Dialogue with History*. Chapel Hill: University of North Carolina Press, 1964.

Yeats Annual. London: Macmillan, 1982–.

Yeats: An Annual of Critical and Textual Studies. Ithaca: Cornell University Press, 1983–1985, Ann Arbor: UMI Research Press, 1986–.

Index

DATE DUE